Young People's
SCIENCE
Encyclopedia

Edited by the Staff of

NATIONAL COLLEGE OF EDUCATION

Evanston, Illinois

Volume 16/Sa-So

CHILDRENS PRESS, CHICAGO

Revised Edition Copyright © 1970
by Regensteiner Publishing Enterprises, Inc.
Copyright © 1963 by Childrens Press, Inc.
All rights reserved. Printed in the U.S.A.
Published simultaneously in Canada.

Library of Congress Catalog Card Number: 67-17925

4 5 6 7 8 9 10 11 12 13 14 15 16 17 18 19 20 21 22 23 24 25   R   75 74 73 72 71

Young People's
Science Encyclopedia

YOUNG PEOPLE'S
SCIENCE ENCYCLOPEDIA

Edited by the Staff of
NATIONAL COLLEGE OF EDUCATION, Evanston, Ill.

ASSOCIATE EDITORS

HELEN J. CHALLAND, B.E., M.A., Ph.D.
Chairman, Science-Mathematics
Department
National College of Education

DONALD A. BOYER, B.S., M.S., Ph.D.
Science Education Consultant, Winnetka
Public Schools, Winnetka, Ill.
Science, National College of Education

EDITORIAL CONSULTANTS
ON THE STAFF OF NATIONAL COLLEGE OF EDUCATION

Elizabeth R. Brandt, B.A., M.Ed.
Eugene B. Cantelupe, B.A., M.F.A., Ph.D.
John H. Daugherty, B.S., M.A.
Irwin K. Feinstein, B.S., M.A., Ph.D.
Mary Gallagher, A.B., M.A., Ph.D.
Beatrice S. Garber, A.B., M.S., Ph.D.

Hal S. Galbreath, B.S. Ed., M.S.
Robert R. Kidder, A.B., M.A., Ph.D.
Jean C. Kraft, B.S., M.A., Ph.D.
Elise P. Lerman, B.A., B.F.A., M.F.A.
Mary-Louise Neumann, A.B., B.S.L.S.
Lavon Rasco, B.A., M.A., Ph.D.

Bruce Allen Thale, B.S.Ed., M.S.Ed.

SPECIAL SUBJECT AREA CONSULTANTS

Krafft A. Ehricke, B.A.E., H.L.D.
Benjamin M. Hair, A.B., M.D.
Charles B. Johnson, B.S., M.A., M.S.

H. Kenneth Scatliff, M.D.
Ray C. Soliday, B.A., B.S., M.A. (Deceased)
Fred R. Wilkin, Jr., B.A., M.Ed.

Raymond J. Johnson, B.B.A., M.Ed.

THE STAFF

Project Editor	Frances Dyra
Assistant Editor	Elizabeth Rhein
Editorial Assistants	Helen Patton Smith, Barbara Ayukawa, Judith Chaffin
Editorial Production Assistant	Shirley Labieniec
Production Manager	Nelson McAllister
Production Assistants	John Andrews, Mitzi Trout

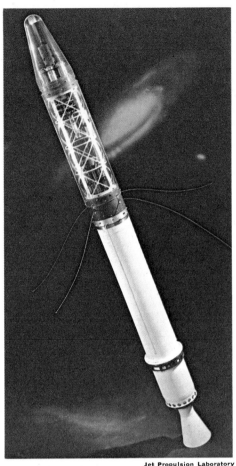

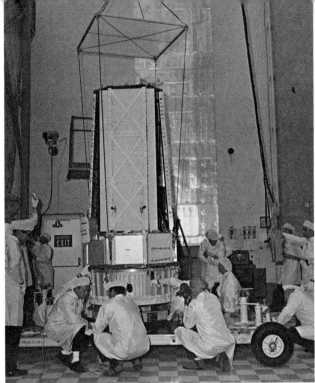

Left, the Explorer I satellite. Above, a general view of the Mariner spacecraft. This spacecraft was launched in 1969 to fly past Mars

Satellite, man-made The first man-made satellite to orbit the earth was launched on October 4, 1957. It was the Russian Spacecraft, SPUTNIK I. Hundreds of satellites have since been placed in earth orbit and moon orbit. Recently satellites have orbited the planets Mars and Venus.

Artificial satellites vary in size and shape according to their purpose or *mission*. Most satellites are unmanned and equipped with sensitive instruments to gather scientific information which is radioed back to ground stations. Some even carry television cameras.

All man-made satellites must be launched by powerful rockets through the earth's atmosphere and accelerated to the high speeds needed to go into orbit.

The speed necessary for a satellite to stay in an earth orbit varies with its average altitude above the earth. At 200 miles approximately 17,500 mph will be required. Only about 6800 mph is needed to achieve a synchronous orbit (in which the spacecraft appears to hang motionless over a point on the earth) at 22,000 miles altitude.

Satellites may be grouped, according to their missions, into several categories, which include *unmanned scientific investigation application satellites, advanced research* and *manned missions*.

The largest number of satellites flown have been those searching out scientific data about the earth and the near-earth space environment.

The *Discoverer* program pioneered the technique of mid-air recovery of packages released from the satellite. *Bio-satellites* are used to study the effects of prolonged weightlessness and space radiation upon living organisms.

An advanced series of *orbiting observatories* are providing a new level of knowledge about the sun, the earth's atmosphere, magnetic field and the surrounding space environment.

A unique achievement in control of satellites were the several *lunar orbiter* spacecraft which were placed in low altitude orbits around the moon.

Applications satellites provide information and services for use in our daily activities. Portrayal of global weather patterns, world wide communications, accurate navigational information and military reconnaissance are examples of coordinated systems utilizing the output of these satellites.

To test and evaluate advanced techniques, materials and equipment for future spacecraft in the actual space environment is carried out on *advanced research satellites*.

Manned spaceflight has attracted popular world wide attention. Small orbiting *Manned Laboratories* (ML) are now being constructed. These will be the forerunners of huge space stations which will be assembled in orbit. R. J. J.

SEE ALSO: ASTRONAUTICS, ORBITAL SYSTEMS, ROCKETS, SPACE STATION, SPACE VEHICLES

Satellite, natural (SATT-uh-lyte) A natural satellite is a body revolving around a larger body in SPACE. The earth and other planets of the solar system are satellites of the sun. Comets and asteroids are also satellites of the sun. Most of the planets, including the earth, have one or more natural satellites. They are called moons.

The path a satellite follows is called its orbit. A satellite is held in orbit by the gravitational attraction of the body it is orbiting. The sun exerts this attraction on all bodies circling it. The planets exert the same force on their moons.

Mercury, Venus, and probably Pluto are the only planets that do not have one or more satellites. Pluto is so small that its gravity could hold only a very small moon. Pluto is so far away from the earth that a moon has not yet been detected.

As the planets revolve around the sun from the west to the east, they carry their satellites with them. Most of these satellites move around their planets in the same west-to-east direction. However, a few satellites revolve around their planets in an east-to-west direction. These satellites are said to have *retrograde* motion H. S. G.
SEE ALSO: MOON, SOLAR SYSTEM

Saturation Saturation is the state of being satisfied or filled. It refers to a molecule with all its atoms linked, a SOLUTION in which no more solute can be dissolved, or a substance which has received maximum magnetization.

Saturn (SATT-ern) Saturn is the most distant of the bright planets as seen from the earth. It is the sixth planet from the sun. Early astronomers believed it to be the last planet of the

PLANET	NO. OF SATELLITES	PERIOD— ROTATION	DIAMETER (If known)	OTHER DETAILS
EARTH	1 (Moon)	.27d.7h.43m.+	. . . 2,160 mi.	
MARS	2 Deimos (outer). . .	30h.18m.	about 5 mi.	Direct motion
	Phobos (inner). . .	7h.39m.	about 10 mi.	Direct motion
JUPITER	12 Ganymede	1d.18h.+	2500+ mi.	May have an atmosphere
	(largest)			4 satellites have retrograde orbits
SATURN	9 (and many tiny masses, associated with Saturn's rings)			
	I Mimas (inner) . . .	23h.	– – –	Direct motion
	IX Phoebe (outer). . .	.550d.	– – –	Retrograde orbit (E. to W.)
URANUS	5 – – –	– – –	– – –	Move in orbits
	I – – –	1.4d.	– – –	Perpendicular to Uranus' solar orbit
	V – – –	13.5d.	– – –	
NEPTUNE	2 – – –	5d.11h.	2240 mi.	
	I – – –	.359d.	about 200 mi. . . .	Retrograde orbit
	II – – –		. . . .	Direct motion

MERCURY, VENUS, AND PLUTO—No observed satellites

solar system. Saturn is one of the four giant planets and is the second largest of all known planets. Jupiter is the largest. Even though the giant planets are very large, they are much less dense than the earth. As an example, Saturn has the least density (0.7 times that of water) of all the planets. It also has the greatest oblateness. This means it bulges at the equator and is somewhat flattened at the poles. Saturn has a system of rings that circle its equator and at least nine satellites.

Saturn can be seen with the naked eye, but it looks like only a tiny yellow speck. Through a telescope, Saturn can be seen to be a multi-colored globe thicker through its center than it is through the poles. The polar flattening is caused by Saturn's rapid rotational speed. Like Jupiter, Saturn has a system of different colored bands. However, Saturn is the only planet that has a system of rings around it.

The rings around Saturn are separated by gaps. The three main ones are called Ring A, Ring B, and Ring C. The outside ring is Ring A. It is grayish. Next comes a gap about 1800 miles wide. This gap is called *Cassini's division,* after the man who discovered it. Ring B is the large, bright central ring. Ring C, the inner ring, is a dark, dusky ring. The planet can be seen through Ring C, sometimes called the *Crepe ring.* The diameter of the ring system is about 170,000 miles. Though it is very wide, the

Saturn's rings are many tiny satellites

system is very thin; it is estimated that the thickness of Saturn's rings is only about 10 miles. Sometimes the rings can be seen edge on, and then they look like a thin line. The rings of Saturn have a silvery-white appearance through a telescope, but the planet itself appears to have predominately yellow coloration.

Astronomers believe that Saturn's rings are actually millions and millions of tiny satellites. Particles of dust, or powder, and small pebbles or rocks are probably orbiting around the planet. The composition of the rings may be very similar to that of a comet's tail. The particles in the rings, therefore, shine only by reflecting light from the sun. The inner sections of the ring system revolve more rapidly than the outer edges do. The theory has been suggested that these particles once made up a satellite of Saturn. Perhaps the satellite got too close to Saturn and was pulled apart by Saturn's gravity. Or perhaps the particles are pieces of another satellite which never pulled together to form a solid body.

Like the other planets, Saturn is tilted on its axis. As it rotates and revolves around

Orbit of Saturn in relation to other planets

the sun, first the southern hemisphere and then the northern hemisphere points toward the earth. When Saturn appears at its greatest tilt, it is at a *solstice*. During the solstices, Saturn's rings are most easily observed. At these times Saturn is viewed from an angle and the rings are visible. When Saturn returns to its equinox, the planet is in a more upright position. Then the rings are seen edge on. Since the rings are thin, at these times they almost seem to disappear. They look like a thin line across the center of the planet's disk. It takes a little over seven years for Saturn to move from a solstice to an equinox position. In another seven years or so, Saturn is at the opposite solstice and the other face of the rings can be seen. Every 14½ years, then, the rings seem to disappear. Halfway between each disappearance the rings are tilted so that the particles can be seen in more detail.

Saturn's average distance from the sun is about 884 million miles. It takes Saturn almost 30 years to go around the sun. Saturn rotates on its own axis in about 10 hours. The different bands of the planet move at slightly different speeds. The equatorial section rotates fastest.

Saturn's diameter is about 75,000 miles. It is 9½ times larger than the Earth. Its density is about 0.71, which is lower than any other planet. Saturn's gravity is thought to be just a little greater than Earth's. Spectroscopic studies reveal that there are quantities of methane and ammonia in Saturn's atmosphere. The temperature of this distant planet is about −234° F.

The discovery of a tenth satellite has been reported but not confirmed. Saturn's largest satellite, *Titan,* is the largest satellite of any planet in the solar system. With a diameter over 3000 miles, it is larger than Mercury. Titan has an atmosphere similar to Saturn's but not so thick. It also contains methane and ammonia. Saturn's smallest satellite, *Phoebe,* is only about 150 miles in diameter. It is the farthest one from Saturn and revolves from east to west. Saturn's other satellites travel from west to east.   C. L. K.

SEE ALSO: COMET, EQUINOX, SATELLITE, SOLAR SYSTEM, SOLSTICE

Sawfish see Ray

Saxifrage see Wild flowers

Scab A scab is formed from pus and serum from the blood. It protects a sore or wound in the skin until it heals. Scab, or MANGE, is also a skin disease of mammals.

SEE ALSO: BLOOD

Scabiosa, or "pincushion flower"

Scabiosa (skay-bee-OH-suh) This is the name for a group or genus of flowering plants. They may be ANNUALS or PERENNIALS. Garden varieties are around two feet tall. Some species grow into twelve-foot bushes.

The common sweet scabiosa is an annual. Its slender stem is one to three feet tall. A row of tiny leaflets grows below each bloom. Larger leaves grow at the base of the stem. Flowers may be rose, blue, purple, or white. Many small flowers form a single dense head. Its knob-headed stamens stick out beyond the round flower top, making it look like a pincushion.

Scabiosa belongs to the Dipsacacea family. They are native to southern Europe. H. J. C.

Scale, animal Scales are platelike coverings found on many kinds of animals. They come from SKIN MODIFICATION or changes on the outer surface of the body covering. Several kinds of scales occur in VERTEBRATES and in INSECTS like the butterfly.

Scales are classified according to the part of the skin involved in their development. All vertebrates have a two-layered SKIN consisting of an inner *dermis* and outer *epidermis*.

Fish scales are formed in the dermis. Sharks have pointed *placoid* scales that are actually modified teeth. They have bony bases, pulp cavities surrounded by *dentine,* and are covered by an *enamel* secreted by the epidermis. Extinct fish had *cosmoid* scales, similar to those on sharks, but flat and like armor. *Ganoid* scales, also armor-like, are arranged in diagonal rows. This type of scale can be found on garpikes. Ganoid scales are formed when the epidermis secretes *ganoin* instead of enamel.

REPTILES, BIRDS, and MAMMALS have horny scales formed by the epidermis. These are surface scales that are shed periodically. Feathers, hair, nails, claws, and hooves are modified epidermal scales. Insect scales are flattened chitinous hairs.   J. C. K.

SEE ALSO: SKIN MODIFICATION

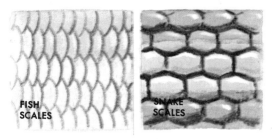

FISH SCALES   SNAKE SCALES

Scale, musical see Musical instruments, Overtones, Sound

Scales see Balance, Weight

Scallion see Onion

Scallop (SKAHL-uhp) Scallops are sea animals with a two-part shell (*bivalve*) that is hinged along one side. There is a winglike extension on either side of the hinge. Below is the *umbo.* Valves may be delicately colored. Deep, radiating ribs on the surface make the edges look scalloped. The two valves are held together by a large muscle that man eats.

Scallops belong to the same class (*Pelecypoda*) as the clams and oysters and, like them, are mollusks. They have soft, headless bodies enclosed in a fleshy mantle. The mantle lining secretes the shell. Both mantle edges have a row of blue eyes called *ocelli.* Unlike clams and oysters, which creep by protruding a fleshy foot, the scallop has a poorly developed foot. It swims by rapidly clapping its valves together.   J. C. K.

Scalp see Hair, Skin modification

Courtesy Society For Visual Education, Inc.

Using a jet action, scallops move through the water

Scandium (SKANN-dee-um) Scandium is a rare metal element. It is barely denser than aluminum, but it has a higher melting point. It has been used recently in making space heat shields. Even though scandium has one of the simpler atomic structures, it is very expensive to purify.

Scandium (symbol Sc) was found in Swedish ores in 1879 by Lars Nilson. In pure forms, it costs about $30,000 per pound. Partly pure oxide is much cheaper. Currently, most scandium is obtained from davidite as a by-product of uranium extraction. Its atomic number is 21; atomic weight 44.956 (44.96, $0=16$); valence, 3^+.   D. A. B.

SEE ALSO: ATOMS, ELEMENTS

Scapula see Skeleton

Scar A scar is usually thought of as a mark or line on the skin that appears when a cut or surgical operation heals. Scars also appear inside the body. If parts of the BRAIN, HEART, or other organs are injured, they will heal with scars.

All organs, including the skin, are composed of specialized layers of CELLS called EPITHELIAL TISSUE. The cells carry out the function of the organ. They are held in place and supported by nonspecialized cells called CONNECTIVE TISSUE. If the injury is not deep, the specialized cells *regenerate* (reproduce themselves), and no scar forms. In a deep wound, all the special cells are destroyed and can only be replaced by connective tissue. A scar results. If a deep wound is in a muscle, the muscle will heal, but the scarred area can no longer contract. Its efficiency is lessened. The same is true of an injured heart. The pumping action is never as great as before injury. A *keloid* is a raised scar that often occurs following a burn.   B. M. H.

SEE ALSO: PHYSIOLOGY, REGENERATION

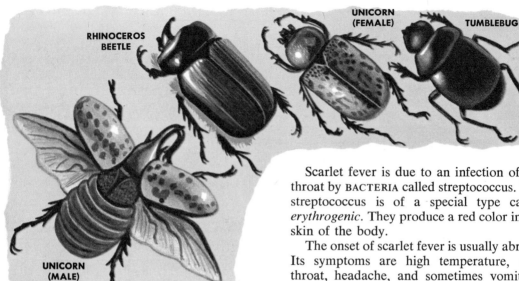

RHINOCEROS
BEETLE

UNICORN
(FEMALE)

TUMBLEBUG

UNICORN
(MALE)

Scarab (SKAR-ub) This is the common name for a family of BEETLES, the Scarabaeidae. Many scarabs have unusual shapes. The males of some species have horns that are used for fighting. Some have legs for digging.

There are vegetation-eating scarab beetles, such as the June bugs and the leaf chafers. There is also a large group of useful *scavengers*. Both larvae and adults live on decaying vegetation or cow, horse, or sheep *dung*. Examples are the *tumble bug* and *dung beetle,* the sacred beetle of ancient Egypt, *Scarabaeus sacer*. This dung beetle rolls fresh cow dung into a ball, pushes it to a chosen spot, and buries it. The beetle then eats it in seclusion. The female beetle lays one egg in the smaller end of a pear-shaped ball of sheep dung. She then closes the opening and buries the ball. When the larva hatches, it feeds on dung until *pupation* occurs. J.C.K.

Scarlet fever Scarlet fever, also known as *scarlatina,* is an acute contagious disease that usually attacks children, especially those from two to ten years old. From one to ten days after a person has been in contact either with someone who has scarlet fever or with someone who is a carrier of the infection (called "strep"), he may become ill with scarlet fever.

Scarlet fever is due to an infection of the throat by BACTERIA called streptococcus. The streptococcus is of a special type called *erythrogenic*. They produce a red color in the skin of the body.

The onset of scarlet fever is usually abrupt. Its symptoms are high temperature, sore throat, headache, and sometimes vomiting. Within two days, a red rash appears on the neck and spreads upward and downward over the body. The rash fades in four to five days with skin peeling. Complications can be serious. Ear infections, RHEUMATIC FEVER, and NEPHRITIS were once common. The widespread use and effectiveness of ANTIBIOTICS has made scarlet fever seem less threatening. B. M. H.

Scarlet tanager see Tanager

Scavenger see Balance of nature

Scheelite see Tungsten

Schist see Rocks

Schleiden, Matthias J. see Schwann, Theodor

Schultze, Max (1825-1874) Max Schultze, a German zoologist, maintained that protoplasm is the fundamental substance of life. He claimed that a cell was the structural unit of protoplasm. In these two ideas, Schultze gave biologists the key to understanding life.

Very little is known about the life of Max Schultze. He was a lecturer at the University of Halle in Prussia and a professor at the University of Bonn.

When he published his paper on protoplasm in the *Journal of Anatomy* and *Physiology* at the age of thirty-six, very little attention was given it. Schultze's paper

Max Schultze

stated that a cell was made up of a mass of protoplasm containing a nucleus. He said that a cell was not surrounded by walls, because if it were, it could not divide, and thus could not reproduce. He also pointed out that the protoplasm surrounding nuclei in different tissues differs from tissue to tissue (and from species to species) because the protoplasm itself has changed, not because of foreign matter in the different cells. Protoplasm is fundamental to life in both plants and animals.

SEE ALSO: CELL

Schwann, Theodor (1810-1882) Theodor Schwann, a German physiologist and histologist, proved that the cell is the basis of both animal and plant tissue. In fact, he showed that the *ovum* itself is a modified cell, as is the *sperm*. He was the first to use the terms *cell theory* and *metabolism*.

Schwann was born in Neuss, Prussia, now part of West Germany. He studied at the universities of Bonn, Cologne, and Würzburg and graduated with a medical degree from the University of Berlin. Schwann first worked as an assistant in Johannes Müller's laboratory at the Anatomical Institute in Berlin. Müller, a physiologist, was writing a textbook on physiology. Schwann helped him to prove the accuracy of every statement included in Müller's book.

Through intensive microscopic study in the laboratory, Schwann advanced the development of biology, the study of life or living organisms. He investigated nerve structure and followed the development of cells in tissue from the embryonic stage to maturity. Although others, including Robert Hooke, recognized the various cells, they did not realize that every animal tissue was com-

posed of them. Since Schwann knew little about plants, he asked Matthias J. Schleiden (1840-1881), a botanist, to conduct plant research. Schwann and Schleiden worked independently on cellular research.

Schwann proved the germ theory of LOUIS PASTEUR when he showed certain organisms could produce chemicals causing fermentation. Schwann discovered that a ferment or *enzyme*, which he named *pepsin*, was necessary for digestion.

Schwann was a fellow of the Royal Society and was awarded its Copley Medal in 1845. M. W. C.

SEE ALSO: CELLS; SCHULTZE, MAX

Science There are many definitions of *science*. One states that science is collected and proven knowledge about the discovery of general truths or the working of general laws.

From the earliest times, science has been the product of man's curiosity. For example, after the Egyptians discovered that they could hammer and shape copper into tools and vessels, their curiosity and needs led them to try to produce a more durable substance by mixing copper and tin. The result was bronze. Through the ages, man has used his senses to observe natural things and events (phenomena). He uses his mind to think creatively about these, hoping to discover how they work. Curiosity combined with observation and thought has produced many sciences.

The sciences may be classified as the *pure* natural sciences, such as chemistry, biology, astronomy, and physics. There are also the *applied* sciences such as medicine, agriculture, and the branches of engineering. These adapt and make use of the findings and laws of the pure sciences. Natural science is also classified according to its subject matter— *biological* or *physical*. The biological sciences study the processes of *life* (plants and animals). The physical sciences study *matter* and *energy* in all their forms. The characteristics and behavior of man and his place

PURE SCIENCE
ALBERT EINSTEIN

APPLIED SCIENCE
THOMAS A. EDISON

in society are the subjects of the *social* sciences. Mathematics is the study of numbers and number relations; it is a tool for all the sciences.

SCIENCE—FROM ITS BEGINNINGS

The Stone Age lasted about 200,000 years. During this period, man learned how to use fire, speak, and make things of stone. He also began to record events, not in writings, but in paintings. In the Metal Age (which began about 6000 B.C. and lasted until about 1000 B.C.), pure science had its beginnings. Man discovered the advantages of the wheel, the use of numbers in mathematics, and how to put characters together to convey ideas in writing.

During the next fifteen hundred years, strong foundations were laid in the physical and social sciences. Astronomy, logic, the mechanics of levers, and Euclidean geometry became well-developed sciences. Then for nearly one thousand years, scientific progress was almost at a standstill. The Renaissance period followed this lull. During this period, which lasted through the sixteenth and seventeenth centuries, higher mathematics developed, Newton's laws of motion and gravitation were formulated, and good optical instruments were built.

The Industrial Revolution, from 1700 to 1900, was scientifically sensational. During this era, the biological sciences were spurred by such ideas as Darwin's theory of evolution, Mendel's laws of heredity, and Pasteur's work on the causes and control of infection.

The physical sciences and technology benefited even more with the advent of the steam engine, the cotton gin, telegraphy, electric lights and motors, the automobile, X rays,

moving pictures, and the theory of radio waves.

In the span between 1900 and 1950, the social sciences made great strides in the fields of psychology and psychiatry. The other sciences also made great progress. The airplane came into wide use, as did the electron tube, television, and radar. By 1905, Einstein had developed his revolutionary new theory of relativity. This theory explained the relationship of energy to matter. Its importance to continuing progress in the sciences cannot be overestimated.

The time since World War II has seen the development of nuclear energy, the transistor, electric data processing, the discovery of the genetic nature of the nucleic acids (DNA and RNA), and many other scientific advances.

LOOKING AHEAD

In every area of science, much more lies ahead. There appear to be no boundaries. As we bombard the atom with more billions of electron volts, new horizons will appear. Space technology is in its infancy. We are just beginning to understand and make use of solar energy. The science of extreme cold, *cryogenics,* is just beginning to develop. The *laser* beam and its companion, the *maser,* promise many practical applications. New fields include communication satellites, ultrasonics, and the new correlating group of sciences called *bionics.* Bionics integrates biology, medicine, mechanics, chemistry, and optics. It is in these and still unknown fields that our future scientists will work.   H. P. O.
SEE ALSO: RESEARCH

Scientific method Generally there are two ways a person can find out how something works, or what the nature of a thing is. He can first develop an *hypothesis,* or unproved theory, and then try to prove the hypothesis right or wrong by experiment and observation. Or he can observe the happenings (phenomena), collect data, and form an hypothesis only after studying the data. The first method is *deductive;* the second method is *inductive.*

Until the seventeenth century the scientist used the deductive method, and it led him into many errors. For instance, suppose he formed an hypothesis to explain a phenomena and the hypothesis was wrong? At the expense of time and money, he had to continue to form and test other hypotheses until he formed a correct one.

In the seventeenth century, SIR FRANCIS BACON, who was influenced by earlier scientists such as Galileo and Kepler, formulated the second method of exploring phenomena —inductive reasoning; and with SIR ISAAC NEWTON, the scientific method as thought of today was developed.

The scientific method begins with *observation*. The observation raises a question, and in order to find the answer to the question, the scientist next performs *experiments*. The scientist carefully records all the results of his experiments in a laboratory notebook. Only after relating the results of his experiments to his knowledge of nature does the scientist formulate an explanation for the question. If the hypothesis still holds true, he forms a *theory;* this resulting theory is continuously altered as new facts point out its limitations. J. R. S.

Sclerosis (sklih-ROH-siss) In medicine, sclerosis is the abnormal hardening of any tissue or structure. In ARTERIOSCLEROSIS, there is a hardening of the arteries. In MULTIPLE SCLEROSIS, hardening of brain and spinal cord tissues occurs in scattered places. In botany, sclerosis is the hardening or thickening of the cell wall of a plant.

Scorpion (SKAWR-pee-uhn) Scorpions are animals related to the spiders (*arachnids*) and found in the tropics or subtropics. By day they live under rocks or in cracks, becoming active at night. Thus they are *nocturnal* animals. They are flesh-eaters (*carnivores*) preying upon insects and spiders. These they tear apart with well-developed pinchers. Larger prey are paralyzed by a sting from a claw on its tail. To man, a scorpion sting causes a painful bite but usually is not dangerous. Only a few can kill.

Scorpions vary between an inch to eight inches in length, and are more clearly seg-

Buchsbaum

Scorpion on a leaf

mented than other arachnids. Head and chest (thorax) are combined into a *cephalothorax* while the abdomen consists of a thick, segmented portion plus a slender, segmented, posterior tail. While walking, it holds the tail over its back.

Its sight is probably poor since its eight eyes are not highly developed. The sense of touch is better developed, the body being well covered with tactile organs called *pectives*.

Scorpions breathe with *book lungs* typical of spiders. The body wall forms thin page or envelope-like folds into an air sac that opens to the outside through a slit. Oxygen exchange occurs in spaces within the folds.

When mating, the courtship ritual is complicated. Young are born alive (*ovoviviparous*) and carried upon the mother's back while immature. J. C. K.
SEE ALSO: ARACHNIDA

Scorpius (SKAWR-pee-uhs) Scorpius is a long curving line of stars that has been imagined to˙ be a picture of a scorpion in the night sky. It can be seen low in the southern sky on summer nights. Scorpius is the eighth sign of the zodiac.

The bright, reddish-colored star that marks the heart of the Scorpion is *Antares*. It is a double star. The name Antares means "rival of Mars." The planet Mars also looks red. Antares is one of the largest stars ever measured. It is so large that it could hold the sun as well as the orbits of Mercury, Venus, Earth, and Mars. Its diameter is about 370,000,000 miles.

Scorpius, the Scorpion

Courtesy Society For Visual Education, Inc.
Sea anemone, or "flower of the sea"

According to mythology, the Scorpion was the animal that killed *Orion,* the Hunter. These two constellations are never seen in the sky at the same time. Sagittarius, the Archer constellation, aims his arrow at Scorpius. The Scorpion is supposed to be responsible for the Sahara desert. The legend says that he frightened the horses that pulled the chariot of the sun. The sun dipped almost to the earth, and scorched Africa. C. L. K.
SEE ALSO: CONSTELLATION, ORION, SAGITTARIUS, ZODIAC

Screech owl see Owl

Screw see Machines, simple

Scrub Scrub is a stunted dwarf tree or shrub, or a thick growth of brush, bushes, and undersized trees, usually growing in poor soil.

SCUBA see Oceanography

Sculpin (SKULL-pin) Sculpin are scaleless fish with eyes on the top of their broad heads. Their eyes have flaps. Their pectoral fins are large and spiny. Sculpin may be either fresh- or saltwater fish.

Scurvy see Vitamin deficiency

Sea A sea is a body of salt water bounded by a mass of land or chain of islands in such a way as to create a more or less distinct basin of an ocean. Dozens of such areas have been given names, but the more important are Barents, Baltic, North, Adriatic, Caspian, Black, Mediterranean, Red, Arabian, Caribbean, Weddell, Bering, Okhotsk, Japan, Yellow, China, Philippine, Coral, Tasman, and Ross.
SEE: OCEAN, OCEANOGRAPHY, SARGASSUM

Sea anemone (uh-NEMM-uh-nee) The sea anemone is a little animal that has been called the "flower of the sea." It has six circles of tentacles (192 in all) around its mouth. As the body lengthens, the tentacles extend until it looks like a flower with its petals opening up. It is usually attached to the ocean floor, but occasionally it will creep on its slimy base. It would probably take a week to move twenty feet.

Sea anemones belong to the Phylum *Coelenterata.* They lack a skeleton, but have a short body which extends and contracts for protection and elimination. The sea anemone has a true gullet and gastro-vacular cavity. It prefers to eat in semi-darkness, and will consume animals as large as fish and crabs. Respiration and excretion occur as the flagellated cells of the gullet sweep water in and out. The nervous system is a simple nerve net found between the ectoderm and endoderm. H. J. C.
SEE ALSO: COELENTERATA

Sea cow The three species of the sea cow, or *manatee,* a plant-eating mammal, have forelimbs developed as flippers, but they have no hind legs. They live in shallow waters.

Sea cow

Maximum high tide   Average sea level   Minimum high tide

Beach

Continental slope

Continental shelf

Approximately 19 years elapse between maximum and minimum high tide

Abyss   Mountain   Trench

Cross-section of ocean and earth's crust showing sea level

Sea cucumber The sea cucumber is an animal that looks like a long, fat cucumber with tentacles at one end. It plows slowly along the mud and sand at the bottom of the ocean. The sea cucumber gets food by eating minute life. When disturbed, it is able to throw out part of its intestine and confuse its attacker. It quickly grows more intestine.

This *echinoderm* has the same radial arrangement as others in the group—starfishes and SEA URCHINS. Five double rows of tube feet make up the WATER VASCULAR SYSTEM. The feet have suckers to help the animal to move around or attach itself to things. The top rows of the tube feet often lack suckers and serve as gill-like respiratory organs. Sea cucumbers also respire by sucking water through the anus (posterior opening) into several respiratory trees.

Blood circulates in a reduced type of open circulatory system. There is no heart. The anterior nerve ring leads off into five radial nerves. This enables one end to find out slowly what the other end is doing.

The sexes are separate in sea cucumbers. Gametes (sex cells) are discharged into the water where fertilization occurs. Bilaterally symmetrical larvae develop from this union.

Sea cucumbers are used as food in China. They are collected, dried, and made into a delicious soup called "trepang." H. J. C.
SEE ALSO: ECHINODERMATA

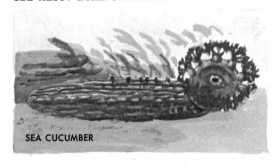

SEA CUCUMBER

Sea level Sea level is the level surface that the oceans and connecting seas of the world would have if it were not for waves, tides, winds, and temperature changes. Because these disturbances of sea level do exist, it is necessary to average the hourly, daily, monthly, and yearly levels in order to determine the *mean sea level* (msl).

Ocean levels are in a state of constant change. Much evidence indicates that the sea level has changed greatly in the history of the earth, especially during the last million years.

There are different things that can and do influence sea level, such as climatic changes and the amount of sediment that is carried to the sea. The most important influence, however, is the buildup of continental glacier ice during the Ice Ages. During these periods, ocean waters evaporate into the atmosphere, condense, and fall as snow on land areas. As this process continues over thousands of years, the waters of the world are stored on land. The mean sea level falls. At the end of the glacial period, the ice on the land melts. The water is returned to the sea and the mean sea level rises. Measurements since 1930 show that sea level has been rising approximately 0.22 of an inch per year, an increase probably caused by the slowly melting polar ice fields. H. S. G.
SEE ALSO: CURRENTS, OCEAN, GULF STREAM, GLACIER, NORTH ATLANTIC DRIFT, OCEANOGRAPHY, TIDE, WAVE

Sea lily The sea lily is a creature that looks more like a plant than an animal. The body is a long stalk with five feathery arms on top. The animal is attached to the floor of the ocean, usually at great depths. It cannot be too fussy about what it eats because it cannot move around.

The sea lily resembles a plant

Sea squirt

Sea lilies have a skeleton of calcareous plates but lack spines. This skeleton makes them one of the most perfect fossils. They were very prolific in Paleozoic times. About two-thirds of the species are extinct now, so the specimens in the seas are scarce today. Currently there are under 100 species.

Feather-stars are closely related to sea lilies, and both belong in the class *Crinoidea* of the phylum *Echinodermata*. The main difference between them is the ability of feather-stars to break loose in adulthood and swim about with their arms.　　　H. J. C.

SEE ALSO: ECHINODERMATA

Sea lion The sea lion is an aquatic sea mammal. It prefers the cold waters of the Pacific Ocean. Related to the common fur seal, the sea lions have long, tapering bodies, small ears, and flippers. They use their flippers to swim very quickly and gracefully while searching for fish. They also use their flippers to get around on land, where they are awkward and clumsy.

The sea lion spends most of the summer days basking on rocky islands where it makes its home. Many performing seals are sea lions. Their fur is not especially valuable.

Sea lions and fur seals both belong to the order *Carnivora*. A related group of seals belongs to the same order but is without external ears, and some members of this group have valuable fur.　　　D. A. B.

SEE ALSO: MAMMALIA, SEAL

Sea squirt The sea squirt is a small sea animal (chordate) which attaches itself permanently to rocks or a fixed object. It can contract its body, shooting jets of water from siphons.

Sea urchin (ER-tchin) The sea urchin looks like a flattened ball covered with sharp, waving spines. Its body plan is much like the common starfish, except that it has lost the arms or rays. When one looks closely at the central disc, this ray pattern can still be seen. Sea urchins live near the rocky shores in marine waters. They eat algae and decayed material.

The urchin does not respond very rapidly to its environment. It moves about slowly by tube feet which project from between the spines on the surface. The fused skeletal plates make the body rigid. Urchins are very colorful, appearing in red, purple, and green. At times they cover themselves with seaweed to avoid being detected.

The sea urchins has five sets of protruding teeth in long jaws. Since it feeds mainly on vegetation, these are useful in chewing. The intestinal siphon is a duct leading from the esophagus to the intestine and bypassing the stomach. The sea urchin has five rows of tube feet radiating upward from the mouth.

Sea urchins reproduce sexually in a manner similar to the starfish. Its power of regeneration is likewise similar.　　　H. J. C.

SEE ALSO: ECHINODERMATA, STARFISH

Sea lions are related to seals

Urchins use tube feet for locomotion

TAKING THE SALT OUT OF WATER

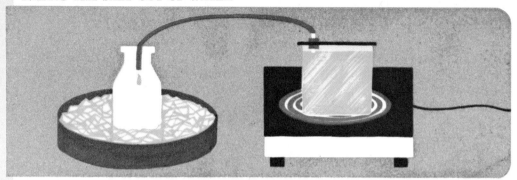

1 Locate a rubber stopper and a container, pyrex or metal can, which can be placed over a source of heat. Fasten a two-foot length of rubber tubing to a short glass tube and insert this into a one-holed stopper.
2 Mix a tablespoon of salt with a pint of water and pour this into the can. Feed the other end of the tube into a bottle which is in a bucket of chipped ice.
3 Boil the salt water until none is left. The salt remains in the can while the water turns to steam. The steam can escape only out the rubber hose. As it hits the cool air in the bottle it condenses and is collected there.
4 Taste the distilled water. Is it salty?

Sea water Sea water contains nearly all the chemical elements. They are mostly dissolved in the water as salts. Sea water not only supports large animals and some large seaweeds, but it also gives support to thousands of tiny plants and animals.

Man is learning to use many of the living things and the minerals in sea water; fish being the first and most important sea resource. Iodine is extracted from seaweeds; and by a long chemical process, magnesium metal can be formed from the sea's magnesium salts. Many sea-coast peoples have for centuries obtained their edible salt by the evaporation of sea water.

The total dissolved salts or *salinity* of sea water is measured as the amount of all salts per 100 (per cent) or per 1000 parts of water. The sea's salinity varies from almost fresh water (near in-flowing streams) up to 4.2% in closed sea basins having nearly constant sunshine and high evaporation rates. Average salinity is 35 parts of salt per 1000 or 3.5 per cent.

Salt makes sea water denser than fresh water. This is one of the factors responsible for ocean currents. In addition, cold

Some Important Properties of Sea Water

Salinity (average)—35 parts per 1000 (3.5%).
　　　　　Density—1.02 grams per c.c.

Salinity (sodium chloride only)—1% to 1.3%

Chemical Composition of Sea Water

Metals	Per cent as solids	Weight (grams) in 1000 c.c. of sea water
Sodium ions	30.0	10.50
Calcium ions	1.2	.42
Magnesium ions	4.0	1.40
Potassium ions	1.1	.39
Other metal ions (including iron, iodine, copper, gold and others)	0.3	.11
Non-metals (in salt solution, with metals above)		
Chlorides	54.6	19.25
Sulfates	8.0	2.80
Bromides	0.2	.07
Carbonates	0.2	.07
Other non-metal ions	0.4	.14
	100.0%	35. (approx.)

sea water—as with all water—is denser than warm sea water. Also, sea water like fresh water requires enormous amounts of heat to warm it. It is because of these two factors—density and high heat capacity—that the extensive areas of the seas affect world WEATHER so strongly. Furthermore, the salts dissolved in sea water lower the freezing point —which for fresh water is 32° F. to about 28° F. for sea water.

When sea water is evaporated by the sun's or by man's artificial heating, only the water molecules go into the air, leaving the salts behind in the body of water.

The particular mixture of the various salts in sea water is very nearly the same as the salts present in the blood and body fluids of plants and animals. For this reason, sea water is sometimes poetically viewed by scientists as the mother of life liquids; and some scientists have developed ideas that all life began in or at the shores of ancient seas.   D. A. B.

SEE ALSO: CURRENTS, OCEAN; OCEAN

Seaborg, Dr. Glenn Theodore (1912-) Seaborg, an American physical chemist, is one of the pioneers of the Atomic Age. In 1951 he shared the Nobel Prize for Chemistry with Edwin M. McMillan. They discovered the element plutonium, named for the planet, Pluto. Dr. Seaborg also won the Enrico Fermi Award (Elements of the Universe) in 1959.

Seaborg was born in Ishpeming, Michigan. He graduated from the University of California at Los Angeles in 1934. He received his Doctor of Philosophy degree from the University of California at Berkeley three years later. Remaining at the university, he became research associate and later a professor of chemistry. Between 1942-1946, he was granted a leave of absence to do research work in nuclear chemistry and physics at the University of Chicago in the Metallurgical Laboratory. Throughout the postwar years, he directed the Lawrence Radiation Laboratory at Berkeley, which dominated the field of heavy-element chemistry.

Seaborg is noted for his work in man-made transuranium elements (elements having an atomic number greater than 92, the number given to uranium). With his associates, he added new elements to the periodic system, using numbers 94 through 103. Number 94, plutonium, is the most widely known because it is used in nuclear explosives. The other elements and the atomic numbers that he and his associates added are: americium (95), curium (96), berkelium (97), californium (98), einsteinium (99), fermium (100), mendelevium (101), nobelium (102), and lawrencium (103).

He has been chairman of the Atomic Energy Commission since 1961. In this capacity, Dr. Seaborg announced in 1967, "The plutonium produced in nuclear power reactors has a massive potential for good or evil. . . . By 1980 enough plutonium will be produced throughout the world each day to furnish fuel for 100 million kilowatt days of electric power or alternatively to furnish the explosive ingredient for tons of nuclear weapons." He is optimistic about the future role of the creative scientist.

Seaborg's articles appear in scientific journals, and he is co-author of *Elements of the Universe,* published in 1958.   M. W. C.

Seahorse The seahorse is a tiny, saltwater animal. It is a fish, although it does not have scales. Instead, it has a hard skin covering. It also lacks caudal or tail fins. Small pieces of skin stick out from its body and look like branches or horns. These make the seahorse hard to see as it hides among seaweed and coral. There it feeds on drifting baby shrimp and plankton.

The seahorse always swims in an upright, or vertical, position. The movement of its fins is so rapid that the fins seem almost invisible. The seahorse swims very slowly and is not strong enough to combat tides or currents. By coiling its tail around grass,

The seahorse is a fish without scales

Buchsbaum

the seahorse maintains a stationary position. It is the only fish with a prehensile tail. When the tail is straightened, the seahorse rises. It rolls up the tail when a lower water depth is sought.

Seahorses, like their relatives, the pipefish, have a habit that is peculiar only to their species. The female deposits the eggs in the abdominal pouch of the male where they are fertilized and incubated. About ten days later, the tiny babies are ejected and immediately swim vertically and independently. The pigmy seahorse produces ten to thirty at one delivery.   J. A. D.

SEE ALSO: TROPICAL FISH

Seal Seals are ocean animals found in coastal waters all over the world. They have smooth, streamlined bodies. Instead of legs and feet, they have flippers for swimming. Seals travel and find their food in water, but because they are warm-blooded animals they spend time on land, too. They return to the land to breed in spots called *rookeries*.

Like all MAMMALS, seals have hair. In some, the hair is stiff and undercoats are sparse or absent. Those with fur valuable to man have soft, dense undercoats and stiff guard hair.

Seals are CARNIVORES, eating fish and other sea animals like MOLLUSKS, CRUSTACEANS, and sometimes seabirds. They have large brains, are intelligent, and rather easily trained.

There are two large orders of seals, those with external ears and those without. Eared seals include the SEA LIONS and the fur seals.

A northern male sea lion may weigh seventeen hundred pounds; the California sea lion weighs half of that or less. Females of the California species are the ones trained for circuses.

Fur seals are about the size of California sea lions, but they have dense undercoats. Sea lions and fur seals are *polygamous*. One large male has a harem of about forty smaller females. The female has one pup a year.

Eared seals are not as well suited for aquatic life as the non-eared group. They

Courtesy Society For Visual Education, Inc.
A family of seals

tend to stay along the shore unless migrating and frequently come ashore to rest. Their hind flippers are adapted for walking on land.

Earless seals are often called true seals. They are more completely adapted for aquatic life. They spend more time in water and often stay submerged for twenty minutes. Earless seals cannot turn their hind limbs forward as eared seals can and when on land, they wriggle instead of walk. Sexes are about the same size; and there are no harems. Females give birth to one pup.   J. C. K.

SEE ALSO: FUR, MAMMALIA

Seaplane A seaplane is an airplane equipped to take off and land on water. It has a hull-like bottom instead of wheels.

The seaplane, or flying boat, has a watertight hull or boat-like fuselage. It rests in the water and is kept upright by small floats suspended beneath each wing. Conventional airplanes frequently have their wheels replaced by two large *pontoons* or floats.

Amphibians are flying boats, or floatplanes, with retractable wheels which are extended for runway landings.

In addition to his ability to fly the plane in the air, the seaplane pilot must be able to maneuver his aircraft on the water surface, taking into account such factors as wind, waves, and currents. A water rudder is usually interconnected to the airplane rudder pedals to provide added control.

A longer takeoff run is required for the seaplane, for it must overcome the water resistance and the suction created when the hull or floats are moved rapidly through the water.   R. J. J.

SEE ALSO: AIRCRAFT, AIRPLANE

Pontoons keep the aircraft afloat

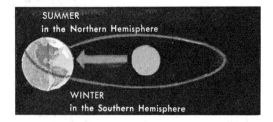

4— AUTUMN
5— WINTER
6— WINTER IN NORTHERN HEMISPHERE;
    SUMMER IN SOUTHERN HEMISPHERE

All photographs courtesy Society for Visual Education, Inc.

1— SUMMER IN NORTHERN HEMISPHERE;
    WINTER IN THE SOUTHERN HEMISPHERE
2— SPRING
3— SUMMER

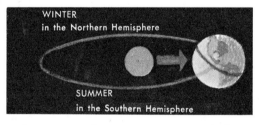

As the earth tilts on its axis, the sun's rays strike the earth to create the seasons; more vertical rays give more warmth

Seasons Seasons are the divisions of the year into spring, summer, fall, and winter. The earth, as it rotates, travels completely around the sun once each year in its orbit. During this trip around the sun, these changes in weather occur.

Seasonal changes occur as different amounts of heat from the sun are received. Because the earth "tilts" on its axis, the North Pole tilts more toward the sun in summer and slightly away from the sun in winter. This tilting is called the *inclination* of the earth's axis. Because of this inclination, as the earth orbits the sun, the sun's rays strike the atmosphere at continuously changing angles. The more vertical the rays, the more heat an area receives. Slanting rays are weaker because they spread the same solar energy over a wider area. They also travel through more atmosphere which reflects some heat to outer space before the rays reach the earth's surface. Another reason for seasonal change is that days are longer in summer. A place is exposed to more hours of sunlight in addition to receiving more direct rays.

The poles experience extremes of seasons: the rays are very slanted, and there are periods of continuous darkness. Places along the equator do not exhibit seasonal change because the sun's rays are nearly vertical all year.

In the Northern Hemisphere, spring begins about March 21. Days and night are then equal in length. Summer commences around June 21, the longest day of the year. Fall starts around September 21, with days and nights of equal length. Winter begins about December 22, the shortest day of the year. In the Southern Hemisphere the seasons occur in reverse order.   P. F. D.

SEE ALSO: DAY AND NIGHT, EARTH

Seaweed Seaweed is a common name used for algae that live in sea waters. Seaweed may be as small as one cell or as large as 150 feet. They are eaten by many sea creatures and man.

The green seaweed usually lives near the surface of the water. The brown variety will attach itself as low as 60 feet in the water with its flattened fronds floating on the surface. A well known brown seaweed is the gulfweed which is found in large masses in the Atlantic Ocean.   J. K. K.

SEE ALSO: ALGAE, KELP, THALLOPHYTA

Seaweed, salt-water algae

Sebaceous gland see Skin

Secretion Secretion is the process of making and separating out special products from the protoplasm of the CELL for use by the body. In a complex body, a group of cells called a *gland* performs this function.

SEE: ENDOCRINE GLANDS, HISTOLOGY

Sedative (SED-uh-tiv) A sedative is a drug that works on the NERVOUS SYSTEM to soothe a person who is nervous or tense. The name *sedative* comes from the Latin word *sedatus,* meaning to settle, calm, or quiet.

Sedatives decrease the excitability of the body when it is under strain or stress. Some sedatives calm an overactive heart; others calm the stomach or the nervous system. Tense muscles can be relaxed by certain medicines.

Bromides, made from the element BROMINE, were prescribed frequently years ago. They are still useful in reducing spasm and controlling convulsions, but they have been largely replaced by *barbiturates.* Phenobarbital is an example. In small doses, barbiturates reduce emotional strain during the day. In larger doses, they induce sleep at night.

Certain *antihistamines* have a sedative effect, although the primary purpose of antihistamines is to control such ALLERGIES as hayfever. A new group of drugs, known as *tranquilizers,* was introduced in 1950. Miltown and Librium are examples. Tranquilizers are useful in the treatment of mental disorders. Still very effective are the older drugs—*chloral hydrate* and *paraldehyde.* These are liquids taken by mouth and useful in alcoholic disturbances. Used in moderation, alcohol is also an excellent sedative.

All sedatives can be dangerous if a person becomes dependent upon them. Excessive doses can produce death by depressing the respiration and producing coma. Overdosage with barbiturates is a frequent means of committing suicide. Sedative action (sedation) can be brought about in many ways without medicines. A warm bath can relax a person, as can pleasant music, a warm drink of milk, and quiet conversation with friends.   B. M. H.

SEE ALSO: DRUGS, PHARMACOLOGY

Sediment Sediment, in CHEMISTRY, refers to solid particles which have settled out of a liquid. In GEOLOGY, sediment refers to a mass of rock fragments which have been carried and deposited by air or water.

SEE: PALEONTOLOGY

Sedimentary rock see Rocks

The sedum is a perennial plant

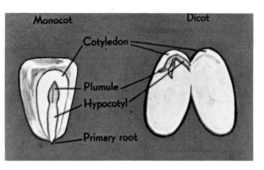

The seed functions as a protective covering and as food for the embryo

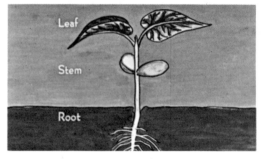

Courtesy Society For Visual Education, Inc.

When the seed is planted, it grows into a seedling, with its three essential organs

Sedum (SEE-duhm) Sedum is the name for a whole group (genus) of flowering plants. They are HERBS or EVERGREENS. Leaves and stems are thick and juicy. Flowers may be white, yellow, pink, or blue.

Leaves may be alternate, opposite, or whorled on the fleshy stem. One species that has no common name is called by the genus name, sedum. It is a perennial for the underground part lives through the winter. Leaves are gray to blue-green. Pink flowers form a dense cluster on top of a foot-high stalk.

Stonecrop is a hardy, upright sedum about twenty inches tall. *Worm-grass* is a creeping evergreen with white blooms only 6 inches tall. *Live-forever* is a foot tall with purple flowers. Sedums are in the family Crassulaceae.   H. J. C.

SEE ALSO: PLANTS, SUCCULENT

Seebeck, Thomas J. see Peltier, Jean Charles Athanase; Thermocouple

Seed A seed is a baby plant with its coat and food. Seeds are all shapes and colors. The seeds of orchids are no larger than a grain of dust, while the seed of a coconut is bigger than a softball. Only the higher plants have seeds. Man and other animals depend upon seeds for food. These include peas, beans, nuts, grains, and rice.

In some plants (GYMNOSPERMS) the seeds are not enclosed in a container. They develop on the scales of a cone. In the flowering plants (ANGIOSPERMS) the seeds develop within a protective covering called a fruit. The formation of a seed begins when the sperm or *pollen* unites with an egg or *ovule*. As it matures, it develops several basic parts. The seed coat (*testa*)

is usually a paper-thin covering. The hard pit of a cherry, the stone of a peach, and the shell of a nut are really parts of the fruit wall and not the seed coat. The seed coat keeps out moisture so that it will not germinate until it has a good place to grow. A little scar (*hilum*) on the seed is where it was attached to the ovary wall in the flower. Near the hilum is a small hole (*micropyle*) used by the pollen tube to reach the egg during fertilization.

Inside the seed the embryo, or young plant, consists of a PLUMULE (*epicotyl*) which are the tiny leaves. These are attached to the *hypocotyl* that grows into the young stem. The lower part of the HYPOCOTYL develops into the primary root. Since the young plant is not green until it is exposed to the sun, it needs to be supplied with food. The food, contained in an endosperm, is stored in one or two COTYLEDONS. Cotyledons are called *seed leaves,* because they furnish food until the embryo is big enough to make its own.

The life span of seeds varies from a few weeks to 1000 years or more. Certain legumes in South America have germinated after 158 years of dormancy. Oriental lotus seeds which were found in peat deposits

✳ THINGS TO DO

WHAT CONDITIONS ARE BEST FOR SEED GROWTH?

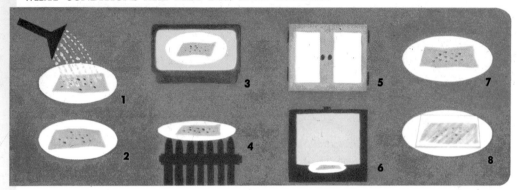

1 Decide upon one kind of seed to use for all experiments. Corn or beans germinate quickly and are very satisfactory for this problem. You will experiment with four different factors: temperature, amount of light, water, and oxygen. It is important to remember when testing one factor to keep the other three factors the same.

2 Select eight dishes. Place a blotter or layer of cotton in the bottom and put a dozen seeds on top of this. Use two dishes for each of the four factors. One dish to experiment with and the other as a control. Water seeds No. 1. Do not water seeds No. 2. Keep seeds No. 3 in a pan of ice water. Keep seeds No. 4 in a warm place. Put seeds No. 5 in a dark cupboard. Put seeds No. 6 in a sunny window. Leave seeds No. 7 open to the air. Place a sheet of glass over seeds No. 8.

3 What happened to each pair? Do seeds grow better in warm or cold places, in light or dark, with or without moisture and air?

in Manchuria are 1000 years old and still good. Some, found in Japan, were dated by the radiocarbon method as over 3000 years old. Whether the seeds of grain found in Egyptian pyramids were still *viable* (capable of growing) has never been verified.

Economically, seeds are vital to man's existence. The food which is for the young plant is robbed by man to feed himself and his animals. Some seeds store mainly starch. Rice has 68% and navy beans, 45%. Sweet corn stores sugar instead of starch. Seeds of LEGUMES rank high in proteins. Those that store quantities of oil are the castor bean, peanut, flax, and sunflower. *Annual* plants depend upon the seed for food storage. *Biennials* need to use other parts of the plant. Since seeds are not produced in the first year, plants such as carrots, beets, and radishes must have root storage of a food supply sufficient to get through the winter and into the following growing season.

Seeds of grasses (oats, corn, rye, etc.) are an important part of the diet of animals, both domesticated and wild. Certain seeds furnish drugs, enzymes, and vitamins. Mustard, caraway, anise, pepper, and celery seeds add spice to man's food. Buttons are made from the ivory found in palm seeds. Every cotton garment worn comes from the fibers taken from the seed coat of the cotton plant. Linseed and coconut oil are used in soaps, butter, varnish, paints, and linoleum. Coffee and cocoa seeds furnish two popular beverages.

It is understandable that most plants must produce hundreds of seeds. Only a few finally end up growing into plants. Man, animals, and adverse growing conditions keep the balance of plant life. If every seed of the dandelions germinated, for example, the world would soon be covered with a yellow blanket.   H. J. C.

SEE ALSO: CAPSULE; CEREAL GRAINS; ECONOMIC BOTANY; FRUIT; PLANT; PLANTS, CLASSIFICATION OF; SEED DISPERSAL

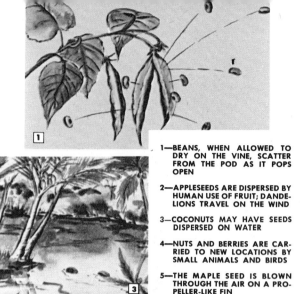

1—BEANS, WHEN ALLOWED TO DRY ON THE VINE, SCATTER FROM THE POD AS IT POPS OPEN

2—APPLESEEDS ARE DISPERSED BY HUMAN USE OF FRUIT; DANDE-LIONS TRAVEL ON THE WIND

3—COCONUTS MAY HAVE SEEDS DISPERSED ON WATER

4—NUTS AND BERRIES ARE CAR-RIED TO NEW LOCATIONS BY SMALL ANIMALS AND BIRDS

5—THE MAPLE SEED IS BLOWN THROUGH THE AIR ON A PRO-PELLER-LIKE FIN

Seed dispersal (dis-PUR-sal) Maple seeds have wings to fly. Cockleburs are hitchhikers in an animal's fur. Linden seeds will parachute to new places. The lotus fruit floats like a boat carrying its seeds down the river to far away places. Some seeds are in little packages which burst open and shoot the seeds out. Seeds are spread by wind, water, animals, explosive fruit walls, and by man—and all these methods are called seed dispersal.

If seeds just fell to the ground, few would survive the crowded conditions. Seeds are contained in different kinds of packages. The seeds on the cones of many evergreens are exposed to permit the wind to carry them away. Many seeds are enclosed in a fleshy fruit. Birds and other animals eat the fruit and in so doing carry the seeds to new places. The seeds of mistletoe stick to the beaks of birds and are deposited on bark high in trees.

Seeds carried by the wind have adaptive structures. The winged fruits of the maple, ash, elm, and box elder are blown great distances. Some seeds have little hair tufts that serve as parachutes, as in the dandelion, goldenrod, and aster. The long epidermal hairs on seeds of cotton, milkweed, and cottonwood aid in dispersal.

The hitchhiking seeds (cockleburs, beg-garticks, burdock, Spanish needles) have barbed dry fruits. They cling tightly to animals and are carried away.

Other fruits have various devices which burst open, forcibly dispelling their seeds. Certain pods, as they dry up, twist and turn, shooting out seeds. Some grass seeds have hairs that move when they are wet. The seeds appear to crawl. It is important that seeds be dispersed or the species would soon die out.   H. J. C.

SEE ALSO: PLANT, SEED

Seedling A seedling is a small young plant grown from seed rather than from a cutting or graft. It also means a tree not yet three feet tall and grown from seed.

Segment A segment is one of the parts into which a plant or animal body is naturally separated or divided. The body of an arthropod, for example, consists of segments which are joined together one after another.

SEE: ANIMALS, CLASSIFICATION OF

Seiche (SAYSH) Seiche is the to-and-fro movement of water of a lake which results in the fluctuation, or rise and fall, of the water level. This happens only occasionally and is caused by changes in atmospheric pressure.

Seismograph (SYZE-muh-graff) The seismograph is an instrument that detects and records movements within the earth. These movements are known as earthquake shocks. The seismograph is a very sensitive instrument, picking up vibrations that man cannot sense. Not only can it detect local shocks, but it can register intense shocks from halfway around the world. The vibrations are traced on a record called a *seismogram*.

The location of the center of an earthquake can be determined by studying the records of three seismographs that are placed at different points on the earth.

A seismograph is so sensitive that it not only detects the vibrations, but gives their approximate location and strength. A seismologist in the United States can locate an EARTHQUAKE and name the location anywhere in the world.

Seismographs are also useful in measuring the depth of icecaps in Polar regions, in prospecting for metals, and in exploring for oil. Scientists set off explosive charges at a certain point, and by means of the seismograph, they can determine the depth and the content beneath the surface at that point. This is possible by the recording of sound waves that bounce back from different rock levels below the surface. Both the measurement of the intensity of the SOUND waves as such, and the measurement of the time it takes for the waves to be returned to the surface are of vital importance.

Because of the variation in the nature of earth vibrations, many different types of seismographs have been designed. The two major kinds (categories) are the *pendulum seismograph* and the *strain seismograph*. The electromagnetic pendulum seismograph is the most widely used in seismograph stations. A coil attached to the pendulum is connected to a sensitive galvanometer. When a vibration occurs, the magnetic field is disturbed, causing motion of the coil. This induces an electromotive force which activates the galvanometer. The galvanometer in turn deflects a light beam which produces a record on photographic paper.

Seismographs are usually arranged in sets of three to record the vibrations in three mutually perpendicular directions: north-south, east-west, and vertical.   D. L. D.

SEE ALSO: DEPTH SOUNDING, SONAR

Selenium (sih-LEE-nee-um) Selenium is element number 34, a scarce nonmetallic element with properties similar to sulfur. It was separated from its compounds in 1817 by J. Berzelius. Selenium burns with a blue flame in air, and reacts directly with many elements. Its principal use is in the manufacture of photoelectric cells. The chemical symbol of selenium is Se.

Two of the six isotopes of selenium, Se^{78} and Se^{80}, make up over three-fourths of natural selenium. Selenium is also used in vulcanizing rubber, and in the manufacture of certain kinds of steel. Selenium rectifiers are important in the design of radio and electronic circuits. The atomic weight of selenium is 78.96.   I. K. F.

SEE ALSO: ELEMENTS

Semen see Reproduction, sexual; Sperm; Testis

Semicircular canal see Ear

Semilunar valve see Heart

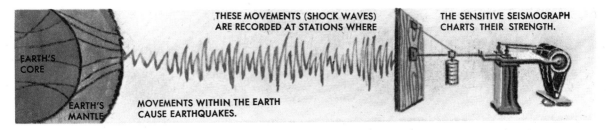

THESE MOVEMENTS (SHOCK WAVES) ARE RECORDED AT STATIONS WHERE

THE SENSITIVE SEISMOGRAPH CHARTS THEIR STRENGTH.

EARTH'S CORE

EARTH'S MANTLE

MOVEMENTS WITHIN THE EARTH CAUSE EARTHQUAKES.

Sense organs Sense organs are special parts of the body that make it possible to see, hear, smell, taste, and feel. For a long time these five were the only senses known. Now man has learned that there are many different kinds of feeling; touch, pain, pressure, heat, cold, hunger, thirst, fatigue, balance, and sensations of motion.

The sense organs report to the body the conditions and changes that are happening (1) outside the body (*exteroception*); (2) deep inside the body (*interoception*); and (3) in regard to the motion and position of the body (*proprioception*). Each of the sense organs is sensitive to only certain kinds of stimulation, and acts independently of other sense organs.

The sense organs register the stimulations, but it is the central nervous system (spinal cord and BRAIN) that interprets the meaning of these stimulations. In combination with every sense organ, there are sensory nerve fibers that carry messages to the central nervous system for evaluation. Through experience and learning, the body is able to react to these stimulations with appropriate, or even intelligent, behavior. For example, if a man sees lightning in the sky, hears thunder, and feels that the air is humid, he knows through experience that a storm is brewing, and reacts by finding shelter.

The stimulations coming from the outside world reach the body through sense organs situated on the surface of the body. The sense of vision occurs when light rays reach the eyes. The sensation of sound is heard when sound waves reach the ears. Taste is experienced as sweet, sour, bitter, or salty sensations when certain substances stimulate the taste buds of the tongue. Odors, and especially those aromas that are

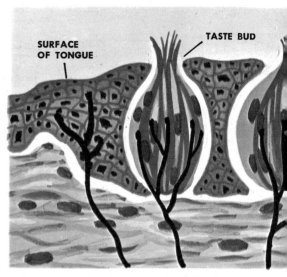

Taste sensation is centered on the tongue

associated with food, are sensed in the nose. There are special sense organs in the skin that detect pressure, heat, or cold. PAIN in the skin occurs when naked nerve endings are irritated.

It is very important that the body have information about its inner workings. Internal sensations which are perceived are only general in nature, however, and do not give as accurate information as the exterior special sense organs do. Hunger is felt when the contractions of the empty stomach stimulate nerve endings. Thirst is the sensation caused by dryness of the linings at the back of the mouth. Pain deep within the body does not pinpoint the distressed area, but merely signals that something is wrong internally. Internal pain is most sharply registered by distention of the hollow organs, as in gas pains of the colon, or spasms (or strong contractions) in the smooth muscles, such as in the uterus at childbirth.

The sensation of awareness of the motion or position of the body is received by sensory end organs in the muscles, tendons, joints, and semicircular canals of the inner ear. This group of sense organs allows the body to judge its own condition in relation to the outside world. The skill of walking a tightrope is achieved by a very high degree of sensory information about the balance of the body and the activities of all various muscles and joints.

In higher animals the exterior sense organs are noticeably concentrated in the

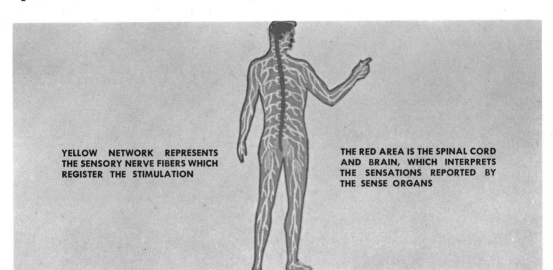

YELLOW NETWORK REPRESENTS THE SENSORY NERVE FIBERS WHICH REGISTER THE STIMULATION

THE RED AREA IS THE SPINAL CORD AND BRAIN, WHICH INTERPRETS THE SENSATIONS REPORTED BY THE SENSE ORGANS

head region and the forward part of the face. In man, other areas of delicate sensation are found in the hand and at the fingertips, making skillful manipulation possible, as well as in the armpit and groin, areas of high vulnerability. The skin of the back is not very sensitive; for this reason it is considered, culturally, the most treacherous act to attack a man when his back is turned.

Lower animals also have sensory organs, but these are usually less well developed than those in animals with backbones. Notable examples of well-developed sense organs in invertebrate animals are the "camera eye" of the squid and the compound eyes and antennae of insects. The sense organs in the simplest animals are arranged in a circle, and give information from all sides of the animal. This is true in the case of the sensory organs of jellyfish.   B. B. G.

SEE ALSO: EAR, EYE, KINESTHETIC SENSE, NERVOUS SYSTEM, NOSE, SKIN, TASTE

Septum see Heart

Sequoia see Redwood

Serpentine (SIR-puhn-teen) Serpentine is a mineral. It often occurs as large rocky masses. Sometimes it is found as grains in rock formations of other minerals. There are two varieties of serpentine. One is a flaky variety that often forms massive rocks. This is called *antigorite. Chrysotile* is a fibrous, asbestos variety. It can be separated into fine, flexible fibers. Specimens of natural serpentine usually consist of a mixture of these two varieties.

Large formations of the antigorite variety can be cut and polished. It is used for ornamentation and building materials. It takes on a waxy luster and often has rich colors. Some of these decorative stones have veins of other minerals running through the green or red serpentine. They look like marble and are called *serpentine marble*.

Chrysotile does not burn or melt. Its yellow or green fibers are woven into ASBESTOS material for fire protection and insulation.

Serpentine is a hydrous magnesium silicate. Its formula is $Mg_6Si_4O_{10}(OH)_8$.   C. L. K.

The two types of serpentine

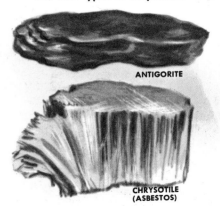

ANTIGORITE

CHRYSOTILE (ASBESTOS)

Serum (SIH-ruhm) Serum is the straw-colored liquid part of blood from which blood cells and the chemicals causing clotting have been taken out. If only blood cells are removed from blood, the liquid remaining is *plasma*. Plasma will clot but serum does not clot.

Serum carries proteins and chemicals such as calcium, sodium, potassium, chlorides, and sugar (*glucose*) in solution. These and other substances are necessary for proper functioning of the body.

The proteins in serum are *albumin* and *globulin*. By a process called OSMOSIS, the albumin keeps a balance between the fluid inside the tissue cells and the fluid in the blood stream. If the albumin runs low in the blood, osmotic pressure will pull water into the tissues, which then swell and produce a condition called *edema*. This may occur in certain cases of NEPHRITIS or kidney disease. It is a frequent occurrence in severe burns and where there is loss of blood and SHOCK. A concentrated solution of albumin is given by transfusion in these cases.

By a process similar to ELECTROLYSIS, the globulin protein can be separated into three main fractions. These are called *alpha, beta,* and *gamma.* Gamma globulin contains the ANTIBODIES of the body. These substances neutralize certain diseases and produce IMMUNITY to other diseases.

People who have recovered from a deadly disease such as TETANUS have antibodies in their blood. Antitetanus serum made from their blood can be injected into another person who has contracted tetanus to fight the disease. If a person has had *hepatitis,* his serum may carry the virus. Transfusion of a hepatitis victim's blood by accident may produce hepatitis in the second person.   B. M. H.
SEE ALSO: ANTIBODY, BLOOD, VACCINE

Sesame (SESS-uh-mee) Sesame is an annual plant grown in the warm parts of the world for its seeds and their oil. The brownish, rounded-flat seeds

Sesame

are used on rolls, crackers, and other baked goods.

Extracted sesame oil, also called *gingilly* oil, is the main cooking oil of India and Central America. Poor grades of it are used in soaps and for fuel.

The plant, *Sesamum indicum,* has small flowers of color varieties from white to pink. Its leaves are oval and pointed. Over three million acres of the crop are grown each year.   D. A. B.

Sessile Sessile refers to a flower or leaf which is attached right at its base and not supported by a stalk. It also describes an animal which is permanently attached at its base and does not move around.

Sewage disposal Sewage disposal of the organic waste products of man and industry is very important in both urban and rural areas. As the population of the world increases, the problems of sewage disposal also increase. Raw sewage can be a threat to public health if it is not disposed of quickly and satisfactorily.

There are many different types of sewage disposal systems. Some are quite simple, others very complex. The type used is usually dependent upon the amount of sewage to be disposed of and the type of treatment necessary before disposal.

In areas where there is no public system of sewage disposal (rural areas and small villages), individual septic tanks are used. In urban areas, a public system of sewers carries raw sewage to a sewage disposal plant. Here it is usually treated in some manner to make it safe for final disposal.

In rural areas, where plumbing systems are installed, waste waters and sewage from dwellings and other buildings are usually deposited in the ground. If the soil and site conditions are favorable, the *septic-tank* system can be expected to work satisfactorily.

The first step in the design of a septic-tank system is to determine whether the soil can absorb the remaining liquid products of the system and at what rate. The soil must have a satisfactory absorption rate without interference from ground water or impervious rock strata below. If these conditions cannot be met, the site is generally unsuitable for a septic-tank installation.

A septic tank allows solids to settle out of a waste and permits clarified liquids to be discharged. The solids are then broken down by bacterial action. The final remaining solids accumulate in the tank and must be removed periodically. The most difficult problem in a septic tank system is the disposal of the liquid remains of the sewage. The most common method of disposal of this liquid is through a network of tiles placed under the surface of the ground. The wastes are carried from the main septic tank system to be absorbed into the soil at another place.

Large public sewage disposal systems are faced with many problems of collection of raw sewage, transportation, treatment, and final disposal. Most cities today have a system of sanitary sewers to move raw sewage and a system of storm sewers to transport run-off water from heavy rains and melting snow. In the past, many cities dumped untreated raw sewage directly into streams, rivers, and other water bodies. Increased population makes it increasingly necessary to treat and break down raw sewage before it is disposed of in some manner.

There are several different ways to treat sewage. Treatment processes are often classified as *primary, secondary,* or *tertiary* processes. There are many different systems that involve a part or all of these processes. The first step in the process involves the disposal of the liquid products. This is accomplished by disposal into a diluting body of water, land disposal (or irrigation), reuse of the liquid to transport solid sewage, or by solar evaporation.

Once the liquid is removed, the primary treatment is started in order to remove the coarse solids as well as the suspended solids. The secondary treatment may involve such things as biological oxidation or chemical oxidation. This treatment serves to further break down the remaining solids. The tertiary treatment makes use of such methods as oxi-

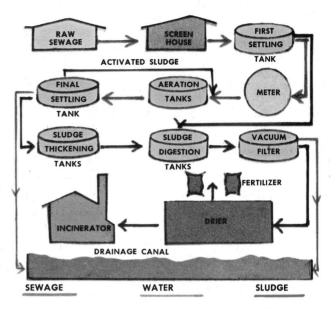

dation ponds, chemical precipitation, ion exchange, and distillation, all of which further break down the solid sewage.

The solid material remaining is often referred to as *sludge*. It is high in many of the natural plant food elements such as nitrogen, phosphorous, and potassium and is often sold as commercial fertilizer. H. S. G.
SEE ALSO: BACTERIOLOGY, SANITATION

Sex Sex refers to the male and female characteristics of plant and animal organisms. The sex of an organism determines the kind of gametes, or reproductive germ cells, it produces. *Males* produce sperm. *Females* produce ova.

Sex determination see Heredity

Sex-linked characteristics Sex-linked characteristics are traits controlled by genes carried on the same chromosome with the genes that determine sex. The genes for these characteristics are always inherited along with the sex genes.
SEE: HEREDITY

Sextant see Navigation

Sexual reproduction see Reproduction, sexual; Reproductive systems

✳ THINGS TO DO

IS YOUR SHADOW SHORTER IN THE SUMMERTIME?

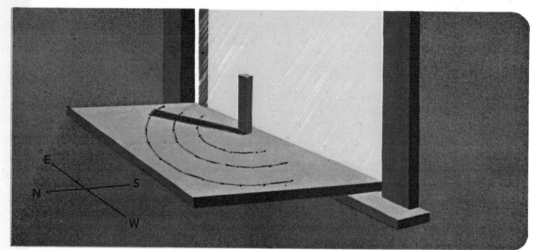

1 You will find it easier to work with a shadow stick than trying to measure your own. The principle is the same.

2 Cut a piece of plywood about 15 by 20 inches. Erect a four-inch stick in the center of a longer side, about one inch from the edge. Place the board in a south window with the stick toward the south and the long sides running east and west.

3 At each hour of the day, make a dot at the end of the shadow and record the time. At night, connect the dots with a curved line. Repeat this monthly to record different curves as the sun reaches higher or lower angles.

4 The higher the sun is in the sky, the more heat we receive from it. Notice that as the shadows shorten, the days grow warmer.

Shad Shad are silver-blue fish found along the coasts of North America. They are about two feet long and weigh up to three pounds.

These hardy members of the HERRING family live in the ocean, but swim up into rivers to spawn. Their eggs are called *roe*. The baby fish that hatch from the eggs are called *fry*. After spawning, the parent fish return to the sea. The fry are left behind in the rivers where they stay until they are big enough to find their way to the ocean.

Fishermen use large nets to catch the shad as they go to spawn. Both the shad and its roe are good to eat. The eggs of the shad are sometimes used as a substitute for the roe of sturgeon in making caviar. D. J. A.

The shad is a North American fish

Shadow A shadow is that dark spot that is formed when light rays are blocked. Its shape depends on the outline of the material stopping the light. Opaque material will not admit light.

Shadows in outer space are clear-cut with sharp edges, since light travels in straight lines in empty space. By contrast, there are often hazy edges to shadows on earth because light reflects from particles in the atmosphere. When light rays glance off objects in all directions, it is called *diffusion*. In effect, this deflection provides light from points other than the true source. The mathematics of analytical projective geometry is used to study shadows.

A shadow in space can be seen on Earth during a lunar eclipse when the moon crosses Earth's shadow. D. J. I.

SEE ALSO: ECLIPSE

Shale see Rocks

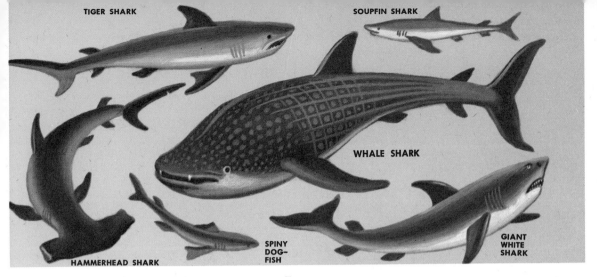

Sharks depend upon both plants and other animals for their food

Labels in image: TIGER SHARK, SOUPFIN SHARK, WHALE SHARK, SPINY DOG-FISH, HAMMERHEAD SHARK, GIANT WHITE SHARK

Shamrock   Shamrock is the common name for several HERBS. (It is the trademark for St. Patrick's Day in Ireland and other places.) The first plant to be given this name was *wood sorrel.*

Wood sorrel has three leaflets to each of its single, alternate leaves. The stem juice is sour from the presence of oxalic acid. Perfect flowers (having both stamens and a pistil) have five yellow, white, or purple petals. They have ten stamens and a pistil of five carpels. The ovary matures into a fruit capsule of many seeds. Wood sorrel belongs to the family Oxalidaceae. White clover and cress are also called shamrocks.   H. J. C.

Shark Sharks are large fish that live mostly in salt water. They are not all the same size. The *dogfish* is only three feet long, but the checkered and spotted *whale shark* is the largest fish known. It may grow to 50 feet long and weigh 15 tons or more. Among water animals, only the true WHALE, which is not a fish, grows larger. In addition to size, the whale shark resembles the true whale in the way it feeds. Small sea animals are strained from the water through many fine teeth.

The giant *white,* or *man-eating, shark* of the warm seas reaches a length of 30 feet or more. The *hammerhead* of the Pacific Ocean has long, flat skull extensions on either side of its head. Eyes are on the ends of these extensions. The *thresher shark* is a large shark with a very long projection from the top or dorsal side of its tail. It uses this to stir up prey by swishing it back and forth among a school of smaller fish.

Most sharks are *flesh-eaters,* feeding upon fish of various sizes. The larger ones will kill and eat sea mammals such as seals and porpoises. A few, as the *nurse shark* in Florida waters, are scavengers feeding upon animal and plant remains.

Sharks belong to the oldest of two classes of fish with jaws. As far as is known from the study of fossil fish, sharks have changed very little from their ancestors. They are quite different from the other group of jawed fish, the so-called *true* or *modern fish.*

Sharks have spindle-shaped bodies, a mouth underneath the head (on the ventral side) and a tail into which the spinal column enters. They have fine open gill slits for breathing and no air or swim bladder for holding or buoying up the fish in the water. Fins are not membranous and are without slender fin rays for support. Their skeletons are made of CARTILAGE instead of bone. The tough, leathery skin has hard, dentine-covered scales (*placoid scales*) imbedded in it. These scales are somewhat like human teeth without the enamel and are often considered as "blueprints" for vertebrate teeth.

Shark eggs are fertilized internally but some sharks lay eggs (*oviparous*), some keep the developing egg inside the uterus without a connection to the mother (*ovoviviparous*), and some have a primitive type of placenta (*viviparous*). In the second and third types, the young are born alive.   J. C. K.
SEE ALSO: FISH, PISCES

Shasta daisy see Burbank, Luther

1533

Sheep Sheep are grazing, cud-chewing mammals. Both males and females usually bear horns. These true horns are formed upon a bony core growing out of the forehead bone (frontal) of the skull. They may be straight or coiled, but they are unbranched. Sheep are in the same family as cattle and goats. Members of this family have an odd number of toes and their nails form into hooves. The female is called a *ewe*; the male, a *ram*; and the young, a *lamb*. About forty domestic breeds are raised for wool and meat.

Wild sheep and goats are closely related and are sometimes hard to tell apart. Male goats have beards, and their horns slant back and then upward. Female sheep do not have beards, and their horns are often curved and spiraled.

The bighorn sheep is a native of mountainous regions in the western United States. They have two-toed hooves, cushioned for surefooted climbing. A pair of spirally ridged horns, flaring out from the skull, curve down and then upward. They live in groups of about six. Females have one or two lambs a year. Dall sheep are large, white animals with widening horns. They live in the mountains of northwest Canada.

The *Karakul,* an Asian wild sheep, is famous for its fur. Fur of unborn lambs is called broadtail; the fur of the three- to ten-day-old lambs is called Persian lamb. The fur of lambs not over two weeks old is called caracul. It is longer and less tightly curled than Persian lamb.

One of the few European wild sheep is the *mouflon.* Although sheep have been domesticated for so long that their exact origin is unknown, most of the modern breeds probably came from the mouflon.

Modern sheep have long tails and very kinky hair called wool. Wild sheep have short tails and stiff straight hair. Selective breeding by man produced the woolly coats and longer tails. Domestic breeds are classified into fine, medium, and coarse wool types. The *Spanish merino* gave rise to the fine wool breeds. Some merino types are bred for mutton. These have less desirable wool than those bred for quality wool. Examples of the medium-wool breed are *Shropshires* and *Southdowns,* bred for both wool and meat. Coarse wool types are the *Leicesters* and *Cotswolds.*   J. C. K.

SEE ALSO: GOATS, UNGULATA

Sheepshead Sheepsheads are food fish found off the coasts of the United States. They are silvery-olive with vertical black bands on their sides. Spines of the dorsal fin are alternately thick and thin. Large incisors help them feed on mussels.

Sheepshead is named for its sheep-like teeth
Chicago Natural History Museum

Shell A shell is the hard, outside, protective covering of various forms of plants and animals. The shells of eggs and mollusks (clams, snails, etc.) are hardened secretions produced by special glands in the animals' bodies.

SEE: MOLLUSCA

Shellac (shuh-LACK) Shellac is refined lac, a RESIN. Applied in alcoholic solution to surfaces such as wood or phonograph records, the alcohol evaporates, leaving a hard finish.

SEE: PAINT, VARNISH

Shellfish see Mollusca

Sheep furnish both food and clothing
U.S. Department of Agriculture photo

Shepard, Alan B. (1924-   ) Commander Alan B. Shepard was the first American astronaut to enter the new realm of space. On May 5, 1961, at 9:34 A.M., he was launched by a *Redstone* rocket from Cape Canaveral, Florida, aboard the *Mercury* capsule *Freedom 7*. Unlike Cosmonaut Yuri Gagarin during his Soviet orbital flight, Commander Shepard had some control over the space vehicle's movements by means of a control stick which activated small gas jets in the nose of the capsule.

Shepard's ballistic ride took fifteen minutes and carried him a distance of 302 miles. Launched at 9:34 a.m. Eastern Standard Time, at 9:39 a.m. his capsule reached an altitude of 115 miles on its arc-like course, and at 9:41 a.m. prepared to re-enter the earth's atmosphere, traveling at a speed of 5,000 miles per hour. At 9:42 a.m. the capsule re-entered the atmosphere and slowed to 340 miles per hour. The drag parachute opened two minutes later at an altitude of 30,000 feet; and one minute later the main parachute opened, allowing the capsule to drop safely into the Atlantic at 9:49 a.m. where it was retrieved by a recovery helicopter. Upon landing at the Grand Bahama Island, Commander Shepard was thoroughly examined by doctors and found to be unharmed. He was later subjected to intensive physical examination on the mainland where his condition was confirmed to be perfect.

Alan Shepard was raised in East Derry, New Hampshire. He was educated at Pinkerton Academy where he excelled in chemistry and mathematics. He then attended Admiral Farragut Academy to prepare himself for the Naval Academy at Annapolis. A very intelligent young man, he scored 3.3 in English and 3.5 in math on his entrance examinations. 4 is a perfect score.

Shepard did not distinguish himself at Annapolis, but his classmates enjoyed his friendly and easy manner. His athletic interests were sailing and skiing. He was an excellent pilot, and after graduation served as a military test pilot.

Always a modest man, Alan Shepard said to President John F. Kennedy after his flight

Commander Alan B. Shepard

that it had been a "very rewarding experience for me and for the people who made it possible." These people were many: scientists, technicians, and skilled workers. Nine thousand private firms worked for two years to put Alan Shepard into space.   D. H. J.

SEE ALSO: ASTRONAUT

Shielding see Nuclear science glossary

Shingles   Shingles is a skin and nerve disease caused by a VIRUS. The virus infects a nerve at its root in the spine. This causes blisters to form on the skin over the path of the nerve. The blisters look like CHICKEN POX.

These painful blisters usually appear first on the back and spread forward to encircle one half of the body like a belt. The term shingles derives from the Latin *cingulus,* which means a belt or girdle. The disease may affect any sensory nerve of the body. Most frequently, it involves the chest, abdomen, or the face above and around the eye. Occasionally, the eye itself is involved. This is very serious because permanent scars may result.

The onset is sudden, usually followed in several days or weeks by pain. Severe pain may last for months after the skin has healed. The causative virus is related to the virus of CHICKEN POX. Except when the eye is affected, shingles is not dangerous.

There is no cure for shingles. The patient is usually able to remain active by taking such medicines as cortisone and antihistamines. People suffering from a serious debilitating disease may develop shingles. Sometimes an older person develops shingles after being exposed to a child who has chicken pox.   B. M .H.

Ships

Ships Ever since the first primitive man found he could float down a stream or across a lake on a log, man has been using boats.

As boats grew in size, the word *ship* came to be used to describe them. Today ships take many different forms. They may be over a thousand feet long and carry thousands of passengers. They may be able to sail around the world under water without ever coming up to the surface. They may be made of plastic, like big bags, filled with oil and other valuable liquids.

Ships may be complete floating laboratories, equipped with every kind of scientific equipment needed to learn the secrets of the sea. They may be filled with huge coils of miles and miles of cable to be laid on the ocean floor, bringing telephone conversations across the ocean.

Man has gone a long way over the waters, and under them too, since those first boats or rafts of logs.

The exact difference between a boat and a ship has never been quite clear. It is usually considered to be a matter of size. All ships are boats, but not all boats are ships. Boats over a certain size are called ships, but just what this size is has been the subject of much dispute.

ANCIENT SHIPS

Ships of ancient peoples were small compared to those we know today, but they were much larger and more complete than simple row boats or even large primitive canoes.

Some extremely large ships made in ancient times were propelled by galley slaves, although there generally were sails, too.

Sometimes these ships had as many as four tiers of slaves on each side, seated on benches one on top of the other, straining at long oars. The oars all worked together in response to a rhythmic call of the stroke. Often the slaves collapsed and died of overwork and harsh treatment.

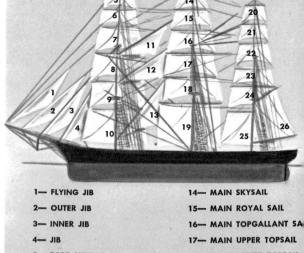

1— FLYING JIB	14— MAIN SKYSAIL
2— OUTER JIB	15— MAIN ROYAL SAIL
3— INNER JIB	16— MAIN TOPGALLANT SA
4— JIB	17— MAIN UPPER TOPSAIL
5— FORE SKYSAIL	18— MAIN LOWER TOPSAIL
6— FORE ROYAL	19— MAINSAIL
7— FORE TOPGALLANT SAIL	20— MIZZEN SKYSAIL
8— FORE UPPER TOPSAIL	21— MIZZEN ROYAL
9— FORE LOWER TOPSAIL	22— MIZZEN TOPGALLANT
10— FORESAIL	23— MIZZEN UPPER TOPSAI
11— MAIN ROYAL STAYSAIL	24— MIZZEN LOWER TOPSA
12— MAIN TOPGALLANT STAYSAIL	25— CROSSJACK
13— MAIN TOPMAST STAYSAIL	26— SPANKER

Galleys of slaves were used even into the Middle Ages, although more effective sails were also used on galleys as time went on.

The most famous operators of ships of ancient times were the Phoenicians.

This small Middle-East nation found that it must have trade from other lands if it continued to exist. So the Phoenicians became the great experts of ships and the sea. Some authorities feel that they even reached the shores of the American continents in their fast, efficient ships.

Another famous group of ship builders was the Vikings. They sailed fearlessly to all parts of the world. Their fast little ships, propelled by oars and sail, were seen in the Mediterranean far from their homeland.

The Vikings, too, are now usually considered to have discovered America, probably about 500 years before Columbus.

By 1492 when Columbus made his first voyage, the design of sails, masts and rigging had progressed to the point where most ships were able to sail efficiently without the use of oars and galley slaves.

Those who have seen reproductions of Columbus' ships know how tiny and helpless they seem, to have crossed the vast stretches of the ocean.

However, the voyages of Columbus greatly encouraged the building of bigger and better ships. This was particularly important

GREEK GALLEY 500 BC.

VIKING SAILING SHIP 1000 A.D.

ENGLISH WARSHIP 13TH CENTURY

SANTA MARIA 1492

"SOVEREIGN OF THE SEAS" ENGLISH 1637

ENGLISH 18th CENTURY GUN SHIP

FRIGATE "CONSTITUTION" 1797

CLIPPER SHIP 1850

to Spain, and so naturally the Spanish took the lead in ship development. Huge Spanish galleons carried the treasures of the New World to Spain.

Because England could not beat the Spaniards in size of their ships, they specialized in trim and speedy ships.

When Spain finally decided to capture England, she undertook one of the biggest ship building enterprises of all time. Her great Armada had huge galleons and galleasses (war galleys), able to carry more than 100 heavy naval guns.

Sails and oars were still the only means of moving ships. But the development of sails moved ahead swiftly. Ships became larger. They used more sails and more types of sails. Sails were placed or could easily be moved to catch every available puff of wind to move the ship faster.

England took the lead in developing sailing ships. One of the most famous sailing ships of all times was the English *Sovereign of the Seas*. This ship was three decks high, for the first time in the history of ships. It was 168 feet long and 48 feet across. The carved and gilded decorations have never been surpassed.

It was not long before America took the lead in sailing ships. Led by the designer Scott Russell, Americans developed one of the best known types of ships ever sailed.

This was the *clipper* type of ship. Clippers were noted for their great speed and were the fastest ships that ever moved under sail alone.

The desire of gold seekers to get to California quickly was one of the principal reasons for the rapid development of the clipper ship. Often the clipper could sail clear around the southern tip of South America and back to the west coast of the United States faster than a party could move overland to the coast. Many Yankee clipper owners also became rich through trade with the Orient.

Up until this time, wood had been the principal building material of ships. Some warships had been covered with iron to give them more protection against enemy guns, but most people felt that a ship made of metal would quickly sink. Of course, this idea was proved false. Ships came to be made of iron, later of steel. Some ships were even made of concrete during the Second World War because they could be poured into shape more quickly than steel ships could be formed. They never proved to be very satisfactory, but some of them are still in use today.

CHANGE TO STEAM

But the greatest change in ships came when it was finally possible to substitute a

Ships

mechanical source of power for men's arms or for wind-dependent sails.

A steam plant was placed in the ship *Savannah*. It crossed the Atlantic from Savannah, Georgia, to Liverpool in England in the unbelievable time of twenty-five days. The year was 1819.

The *Savannah* also had masts and sails. For a good many years after the first Atlantic crossing of a steamboat, boats had both power plants and sails. If something should happen to the steam plant, the sails would still be reliable. Also, the steam engines were not very efficient, and sails added to the speed.

The first steamships all used paddle wheels on the sides to push the ships through the water.

When the principle of the screw type propeller was adopted, it was found to be much more satisfactory. The great propellers in some of the largest modern ships are several stories high, and there may be as many as four propellers on a single ship.

Other improvements came. The methods of bringing steam power from the boiler to the paddles or propeller were constantly being made more efficient, and the types of engines improved. Piston engines were developed followed by engines using the TURBINE principle.

Many modern ships still depend on the power of steam, but some of them use the steam to generate electricity to power electric motors which turn the propellers.

All of these engines required the use of boilers to generate steam to operate the machinery in one manner or another.

Then a German inventor named Diesel created an engine which takes its thrust from the firing of oil in the cylinder itself.

It was not long before this type of *internal combustion* engine was being tried in ships, and motor ships with diesel engines have become increasingly popular and efficient. They require less storage space for fuel, and they are more economical in their fuel requirements.

Many ships use their diesel engines to power electric generators which turn the propellers.

Others apply the power of the diesel cylinders directly to gearing arrangements which turn the screws.

NUCLEAR SHIPS

The most modern developments in power

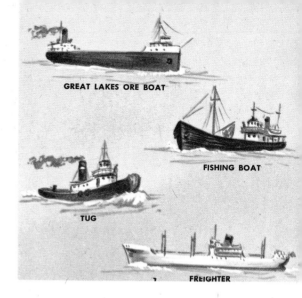

GREAT LAKES ORE BOAT

FISHING BOAT

TUG

FREIGHTER

plants for ships are probably more amazing than any other in the history of ships. An engine has been developed which uses the heat of NUCLEAR ENERGY to fire the boilers of a wholly new kind of steamship—the so-called "nuclear ship."

The most important facts of this development are the small size of the fuel necessary and the tremendous mileage that can be covered before a nuclear ship must be refueled. The exact size of atomic or fissionable material required to keep a ship in operation for many months is not generally known, but some officials have hinted that its size may not be much larger than that of a baseball.

Certainly when it is considered how much space is need for the oil or coal used by a conventional engine for a single voyage, the advantages of nuclear power are very clear.

Because submarines have special problems with regular fuels, the first ships developed by the United States with nuclear power were underwater craft.

Russia's first nuclear ship was a heavy icebreaker. Russia and the United States are developing both warships and commercial ships using atomic fired steam generators.

A number of technical terms are commonly used in connection with ships. The term *beam* refers to the width of a ship. *Displacement* is a term referring to the amount of water which is displaced by the ship and is one of the means of measuring the total weight of the ship and its load.

Designers of ships must keep in mind the type of use a ship will have in creating its shape and structure.

Passenger ships must have speed and comfort for the passengers. They are usually of great size to carry the largest possible

CLERMONT 1807

SAVANNAH 1819

GREAT EASTERN 1862

VIRGINIA AND THE MONITOR
(MERRIMAC) 1862

UNITED STATES 1951

USS TRITON 1960
(ATOMIC)

HYDROFOIL 1958

SAVANNAH 1959
(ATOMIC POWERED)

payload and to accommodate swimming pools and the other features which appeal to ocean travelers. The passenger liner is said to be increasing again in popularity after losing for a time to the passenger airplane.

Stability of a passenger ship is one of its most important qualifications. New devices are constantly being worked out to keep ships from rolling and swaying, and some of the new methods have been applied with great success.

Cargo ships are generally slower and are built to carry the greatest possible load for their size. Special ships are developed for special cargoes, such as the refrigerated ships which carry perishable produce.

THE FUTURE

It appears that *hydrofoil* ships will be used increasingly in the future. These are ships with thin fins on the sides. When the ship develops sufficient speed, the hull rises out of the water, much as the wings of an airplane makes it rise in the air. Friction of the water is greatly reduced, making possible much greater speeds.

It was at first thought that hydrofoil development would be restricted to smaller ships, but now it is used on larger craft.

Another possible future development is the "air effect" or air-cushion vehicle. This flat-bottomed craft rises a short way above the water on a cushion of air. Forward motion is accomplished with a jet engine or air propeller.

The largest ships ever built in the history of shipping are those now in use as United States aircraft carriers of the *Forrestal* class. These ships, blocks long, have flight decks the size of many football fields and have the population and living facilities found in me-dium-sized cities.

Ships built for research are exploring the Arctic and Antarctic. Other ships are floating laboratories investigating animal or mineral life of the sea. J. A. C.

SEE ALSO: AIR-CUSHION VEHICLE, BOATS EN-GINES, SUBMARINES

Shivering Shivering is a slight shaking of the body, due to a contraction or twitching of a group of muscles. It occurs when the body is exposed to cold, or as a result of fear or disease.

Shock Shock is a term used to describe a sudden mental or physical disturbance. An electric shock results from making contact with electric wires. The nerves of the body are used as conductors. If the current is great, the heart can stop beating.

A severe emotional experience, such as fright or the sudden death of a friend or family member, can produce shock by nervous action on the PITUITARY gland. Sudden loss of blood (hemorrhage), a severe crushing injury to a body muscle, or a heart attack can also cause shock. Overwhelming infections, such as blood poisoning, can cause shock. *Anaphylactic* shock occurs when a substance that the body is sensitive to is injected into it.

Shock is characterized by a rapid, feeble pulse; cold, clammy, moist, colorless skin; a low blood pressure; and subnormal temperature. Treatment is by intravenous fluids. Blood or plasma is sometimes given. Drugs to raise the blood pressure, ACTH, and COR-TISONE are useful. B. M. H.

SEE ALSO: FIRST AID, STRESS

Shooting star see Meteor

1539

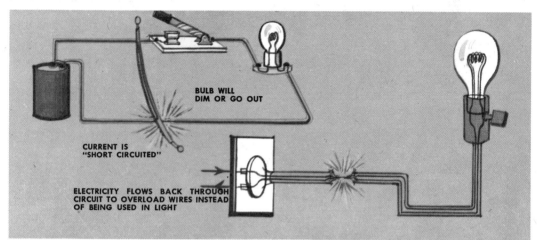

BULB WILL
DIM OR GO OUT

CURRENT IS
"SHORT CIRCUITED"

ELECTRICITY FLOWS BACK THROUGH
CIRCUIT TO OVERLOAD WIRES INSTEAD
OF BEING USED IN LIGHT

Short circuit (SUR-kit) An electric circuit is the path that an electric current takes. The current flows from one side of the source through a conductor, such as a wire, through a resistance, such as an appliance, to the other side of the source. A short circuit occurs when the current finds a path without resistance. Then large amounts of current flow and can burn insulation and start a fire.

Short circuits are often caused by two wires touching each other when they are supposed to be separated. Loose connections in a socket or broken or worn-out insulation in cords can allow the wires to touch. A nail, or pin, or screwdriver inserted into a socket can also cause a short circuit—and a severe burn, or worse, to anyone touching it.

Ordinarily the circuit followed by the current takes it through certain resistances which oppose the current flow. The heat generated by the work done in overcoming this resistance, in an electric light bulb filament or a toaster for example, makes the filament glow or the toaster heat. When two sides of the electric circuit are accidentally connected by a path which cuts out this resistance, a short circuit occurs. Electric current always flows through the path of least resistance, thus large amounts of current will flow and the wire gets too hot.

Fuses are safety devices that help to prevent fires that could be caused by overloaded circuits and short circuits. When a circuit is overloaded or shorted, the fuse blows out. Fuses are made of a lead alloy that has a low melting point. When an excess amount of heat is generated, the alloy melts and stops the flow of current. A fuse must never be replaced with a penny or wire.   C. L. K.
SEE ALSO: ELECTRICITY, FUSE

Short wave radio Short wave radio is a means of communication which can link distant points with voice, code, or teletype.

The short wave band is a range of radio frequencies from 1700 to 30,000 kilocycles which provide reliable communication at distances from 1000 to 12,000 miles over the earth's surface. This important band carries long distance telephone links, provides government and military services with instantaneous channels of command, and connects the news services of the world with most of their foreign sources. Short wave radio is the only effective means of emergency and distress communication for ships, planes, and isolated areas. It is compulsory equipment on all ships.

GUGLIELMO MARCONI (1874-1937) made the first experiments in long-distance communication in 1901 when he sent a radio signal across the Atlantic. Heinrich Hertz had earlier shown that radio waves were electromagnetic in nature, similar to light waves but with a much longer wave length. Like light, radio waves travel in a straight line unless they are reflected or refracted. In 1902, two scientists working independ-

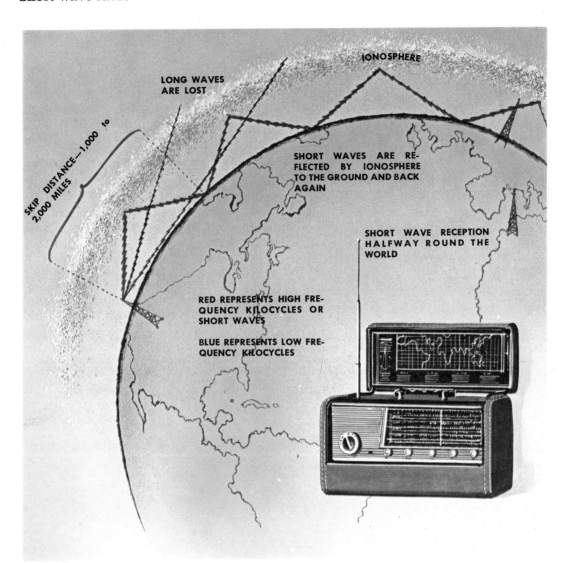

IONOSPHERE

LONG WAVES
ARE LOST

SKIP DISTANCE—1,000 to
2,000 MILES

SHORT WAVES ARE RE-
FLECTED BY IONOSPHERE
TO THE GROUND AND BACK
AGAIN

SHORT WAVE RECEPTION
HALFWAY ROUND THE
WORLD

RED REPRESENTS HIGH FRE-
QUENCY KILOCYCLES OR
SHORT WAVES

BLUE REPRESENTS LOW FRE-
QUENCY KILOCYCLES

ently, Arthur Kenelly and Oliver Heaviside, were able to explain why long-distance radio transmission was possible. Their theory was that a layer of the earth's upper atmosphere, called the *ionosphere,* is electrically charged by the sun's radiation. The ionosphere can bend short radio waves back to earth. This explains why radio signals can be received over thousands of miles instead of being cut off by the horizon.

Early radio operators used the long waves, or low frequencies, and believed that the high frequencies or shorter wave lengths, were not so dependable. In 1921 many amateur operators, called *hams,* on both sides of the Atlantic began to experiment with reliable low-cost communications across the ocean. They discovered that the "skip" of radio waves from the ionosphere is more de-

pendable at shorter wave lengths, and that they were often reflected again from the ground to the ionosphere, in 1,000 to 2,000 mile skips which could circle the earth.

By 1930, the British Commonwealth used a short wave radio network to link London to India and to Australia. In 1932, experimental television transmissions were made from London using very high frequencies. Within a few years before World War II, both short-wave television and short-wave voice broadcasting were developed and used in the United States and England. Today, practically every nation makes short-wave broadcasts of music, news, and information to listeners all over the world.   D. A. B.

SEE ALSO: ATMOSPHERE, ELECTROMAGNETIC SPECTRUM, ELECTRONICS, RADIO, SOUND, SOUND INTERFERENCE

Shrews must eat continually to keep alive

Shrew The shrew is the smallest mammal in the world but one of the mightiest. It will fight animals twice its size. Some adults weigh less than a peanut. What a delicate scale one would need to weigh a baby shrew. Shrews spend most of their short lives looking for and eating food. They feast upon insects, small mollusks, and tiny rodents. When these tasty animals can't be found, a shrew will even eat another shrew.

This timid little animal lives on or in the ground. It is seldom seen since it is usually nocturnal. They have several broods each year with the offspring numbering up to ten. Shrews have fine soft fur which hides their tiny eyes that most likely see only dark and light forms. Their snout is almost as sharp and pointed as their teeth. The body has a musky smell which serves somewhat as a protection against other animals. Some shrews have scaly tails and some have poisonous saliva which paralyzes when injected in another animal.

Shrews are the most primitive of the placental mammals, being related to early primates. They are classified in order *Insectivora* with the moles and hedgehogs. They are found all over the world except in Australia. About 25 species have been found in the United States.   H. J. C.
SEE ALSO: INSECTIVORE, MAMMALIA

Shrike A shrike is a small BIRD OF PREY about the size of a robin. It has the habits of a hawk and the feet of a songbird. It is the only hawklike bird

Shrike is sometimes called "butcher-bird"

that sings. Another name for the shrike is sparrow hawk.

Shrikes are gray, black, and white. Their wings and tail are black; a black mask marks their eyes. The upper body is gray and the lower part is white. The upper bill has a sharp, strong hook and is black; the lower bill is flesh-colored where it joins the head. When they fly they stay low to the ground with much flapping of their wings.

Shrikes feed upon insects, mice, and English sparrows. Since they lack claws for grasping prey, they chase prey until it is fatigued, and then impale it upon spikes, thorns, fence barbs, or forked branches. For this reason, the shrike is often called the "butcherbird."

The shrike builds an open nest, and the female lays four or five mottled gray eggs.
                                              J. C. K.

SEE ALSO: BIRDS OF PREY

Shrimp The common shrimp is a small, lobster-like animal. The limy, thin, outside skeleton (so-called "shell") is flattened sidewise, and colored to blend with the ocean floors near coasts where they live and hide from man's nets. The edible shrimps grow to three inches long. Others are longer legged with smaller bodies.

A shrimp breathes by gills hidden in its sides. It swims by bending its abdomen which, in turn, moves its large tail fin. It walks on legs attached to the middle of its body, and feels with its long antennae. It feeds on small sea animals and plants.

Fresh water shrimp are not really shrimp, but amphipods. Some may reach a length of ½ inch. They have high arched backs and are colored greenish-white to brown. They are important sources of food in fish hatcheries, but are too small to be eaten by man. The female lays about twenty eggs every eleven days, and incubates them in a brood sac attached to its underside. The mated pairs

The shrimp's skeleton wraps around its body
Courtesy Society For Visual Education, Inc.

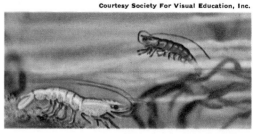

continue to swim together. Amphipods use their numerous posterior legs to swim backwards and upside down.

The shrimp industry is important along the southern coasts of the United States. Six-inch shrimps, found on the Pacific coast and Gulf coast, are called *prawns*.   P. G. B.

SEE ALSO: CRUSTACEA

Shrub   Shrubs are woody, bushy plants that continue growth after the first year. Their stems are often slender and exhibit much branching near the ground.

Shrubs form one of the three groups into which all higher plants are divided. The other two groups are HERBS and TREES. The divisions of the groups can be seen in their external pattern of plant parts. Herbs are often green above the ground with little or no increase in the stem's diameter. They have soft stems. A tree is a wood plant, generally much larger than a shrub, and often with one main trunk. Branches on trees are usually nearer the top.

Some plants may be herbs in temperate regions but shrubs in tropical areas. Geranium is an example. In northern states, it is grown outside as an ANNUAL. Freezing prevents any new growth. However, geraniums grown in warm climates lay down wood cells, and live as PERENNIALS. They may develop into shrubs many feet high.

Some plants may be either shrubs or trees. This depends upon the method of pruning. Certain yews and junipers are good examples. If in the first couple of years of growth the terminal buds are pruned or cut off, the lateral buds on the first stem near the ground will develop. They grow out and up to form lateral branches. Constant pruning will cause the plant to become a low, many-branched shrub. However, if the terminal buds are permitted to grow undisturbed, a main trunk will form. The plant then becomes a tree rather than a shrub.

Courtesy Society For Visual Education, Inc.

F. A. Blashfield

(Top) Wild rose

(Second) Sumac

(Third) Hibiscus

(Bottom) Pussy willow

F. A. Blashfield

Courtesy Society For Visual Education, Inc.

SPRING-FLOWERING SHRUBS

Shrubs that flower early in March and during the spring are very welcome after the winter. They are well known for their colorful and often fragrant blossoms. Among them are the witch-hazels with bright, yellow flowers; the flowering quince; jasmine with fragrant white or yellow blossoms; the popular honeysuckles; Prinsepia with small yellow flowers; and forsythia, its yellow flowers among the earliest to open.

SUMMER AND LATE-FLOWERING SHRUBS

The display of flowering shrubs may be carried on throughout the summer months and into the fall by a careful selection of shrubs. The spiraeas bloom in early summer. The Scotch broom and related varieties have attractive yellow flowers. Other late-flowering shrubs are Chinese Abelia, sweet-scented Buddleia, summer sweet, rose-of-Sharon, hydrangea, mock-orange, and lilacs.

SHRUBS THAT ARE COLORFUL IN FALL AND WINTER

Many shrubs have colored stems and twigs, and add color to the garden after the foliage has disappeared. These shrubs often do best when planted near water. In some, the color deepens as winter goes on, and spring approaches. They have the brightest coloring when they are planted in open areas. Various dogwoods and willows have brilliant yellow and red branches and stems. Barberry has colorful leaves in the fall, and orange-red berries, and colorful stems.

SHRUBS WITH COLORFUL FRUIT

These shrubs are gaining in importance as specimen plants. They keep their colorful fruit long after the growing season, and sometimes all winter. Shrubs of Berberis (barberry), Cotoneaster, Cornus (dogwood), Cuonymus, Ilex (holly), Lonicera (honeysuckle), Ligustrum (privet), and Vibernum have many species that produce colorful fruit. Some Callicarpa have lilac- or violet-colored fruit. Many sumacs and the spice-bush have a reddish fruit.

SHRUBS THAT THRIVE IN ACID SOILS

Most shrubs cannot tolerate acid soils, but there are some that require it. Some of the most beautiful shrubs need acid conditions. The best known of these are members of the heath family, especially the rhodo-

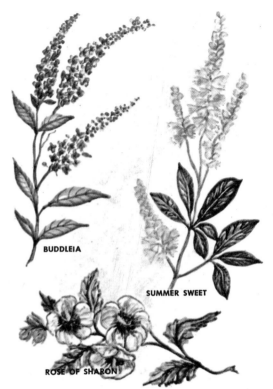

BUDDLEIA

SUMMER SWEET

ROSE OF SHARON

dendrons. Others are the azalea, magnolia, spice-bush, yew, blueberry, and spruce.

SHRUBS THAT THRIVE IN DRY ROCKY AREAS

These are very important shrubs. They are mainly wild, native shrubs, such as the blueberry, wild raspberry, and wild roses.

SHRUBS FOR BORDERS OR HEDGES

A border or hedge of shrubs is considered a permanent planting. It is pruned and trimmed to the desired height, which will make it compact and dense. Hedges need careful thinning out of the older parts, and regular feedings. Evergreen hedges may include such plants as yew, cedar, spruce, arborvitae, and some varieties of holly. Deciduous hedges that will be trimmed to shape may include such shrubs as osage-orange, privet, flowering quince, buckthorn, and some kinds of hawthorn.

SHRUBS THAT THRIVE IN SHADY SPOTS

Sometimes shrubs are needed in shaded places. Many will do well in such a location —Forsythia, Ligustrum, some viburnums, and deciduous kinds of euonymus.

BROAD-LEAVED EVERGREENS

These shrubs are well worth the special care they require. Most of them prefer a

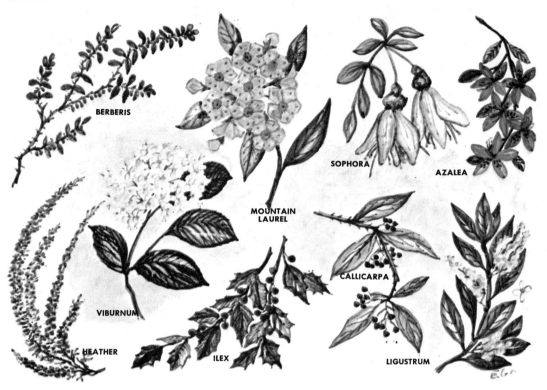

BERBERIS

SOPHORA

AZALEA

MOUNTAIN LAUREL

CALLICARPA

VIBURNUM

HEATHER

ILEX

LIGUSTRUM

sheltered and partly shaded location. Only a few of the broad-leaved evergreens are hardy in the north. Among them are some rhododendrons, mountain-laurel, heather, native sand-myrtle, and some species of euonymus.

FINEST FLOWERING SHRUBS IN THE
UNITED STATES

The flame AZALEA is considered by many to be the finest ornamental shrub of the United States. It has a gorgeous display of beautifully colorful flowers. The San Diego Fremontia is another outstanding shrub, because of its beauty, its great profusion of flowers, its fine shape, and its beautiful individual flowers. Another very fine shrub is the mescalbean, Sophora. It has very attractive foliage, exquisite fragrance, and beautifully colored, showy flowers. Others are the cranberry-bush, the white fringetree, and the mountain-laurel Kalmia.   M. R. L.

SEE ALSO: FERTILIZER, GARDENING, PRUNE

Shunt see Ammeter

Siamese fighting fish see Tropical fish

Sidereal day see Earth

Sierra Nevadas see North America

Sigma see Statistics

Silage Silage is vegetation, such as cornstalks, cut and preserved for winter feed for animals in a chamber called a silo. It stays moist and ferments because of the action of fungi.

Silicon (SILL-uh-kuhn) Silicon is the second most abundant element. It is never found free in nature. Silicon, chemical symbol Si, has an atomic number of 14.

Pure silicon is a gray solid, very brittle and markedly metallic in appearance. It is produced by the reduction of silicon dioxide or silica, SiO_2.

$$SiO_2 + 2C \rightarrow Si + 2CO$$

Silicon is used in the making of glass and the casting of steel and copper. It increases steel's resistance to corrosion. In the last ten years silicon has gained wide use in the production of solar batteries.

Silicon exists in different crystal compounds, of which QUARTZ is most common. It is useful for its high melting point, 1600°C.; low heat expansion; and transparency to ultraviolet. Its atomic weight is 28.086 (28.09, O = 16).

E. Y. K.

SEE ALSO: ELEMENTS, GLASS, SILICON LIFE

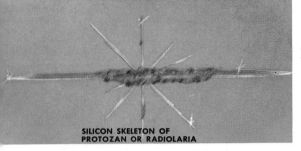

Diatoms represent Earth's silicon life

Silicon life Life on the planet Earth is based on carbon as the main element. Nothing is known about life on other worlds, but an interesting question arises when thinking about such life. Is this life based on carbon or is it possibly based on another element?

The outstanding feature of carbon life is its capability to form molecular combinations with many other elements, especially hydrogen, and to build a variety of molecular structures as well as complex structures. This ease with which carbon combines with other elements is one of the chief causes of the great stability and versatility of carbon life. In a search for other elements of similar qualifications, not much choice is found.

The only element that even remotely resembles carbon in this respect is SILICON. Next to carbon, silicon is capable of entering more molecular combinations than any other element, but these are still only a small number compared to those formed by carbon.

Silicon occupies as important a position in the universal world as carbon does in the world of plants and animals. Its chemistry is based on the combination of silicon dioxide (SiO_2) with other oxides. Hydrogen compounds similar to those of the simpler carbon-hydrogen compounds are formed; for example, in methane (CH_4) the carbon atom can be replaced to form silico methane (SiH_4) or, in ethane (C_2H_6) both carbon atoms can be replaced by silicon atoms to give silico-ethane. The hydrogen compounds of silicon, however, are far less stable than the corresponding carbon compounds.

Free silica (SiO_2) and silica in combination with other oxides form approximately 6% of the earth's crust. It is used by some plant and animal life; for example, the hard surface and the sharp edges of some grasses are due to silica. The skeletons of tiny marine animals, the DIATOMS, are made of silica. But nowhere on this planet does silicon replace carbon as the basis of organic life processes.

By silicon life is meant living organisms in which the key role is played by silicon atoms rather than by carbon atoms. Is such life *possible?* This is not known. Under certain, rather restrictive conditions, such life might have a chance to develop.

Is it likely silicon life will be found on other planets? The answer to this question appears to be no. It is far more likely carbon life will be found. This has several reasons. One is that silicon is far more partial to oxygen than carbon. A silicon-hydrogen compound is rapidly destroyed by oxygen. Another important reason is that many of the compounds of silicon are solid while those or similar ones of carbon are liquid or gaseous. This imposes a severe restriction on the development of such fine regulatory capabilities as they are provided by the hormones, for example, which are complex chemicals which among other things, regulate the growth, reproductive capabilities. The milk glands in animal life also are growth regulators and stimulators of flowering processes in plants.

Another important function of certain plant HORMONES, the so-called *wound* hormones, is to stimulate a rapid division of cells in the vicinity of wounds, causing the formation of tissue to close the wound. Chemical evidence indicates that silicon atoms could not form stable compounds of the complexity of the hormones or even of the carbohydrates which form another vital part of carbon life. The carbohydrates are a great variety of sugars (for example, glucose or "grape sugar," $C_6H_{12}O_6$ or cane sugar, $C_{12}H_{22}O_{11}$) and non-sugars (for example, starches and celluloses). The most important carbohydrate is glucose, formed by photosynthesis as described below. All sugar carbohydrates are soluble in water, whereas the non-sugars are insoluble in water.

This leads to the third basic reason for the lesser probability of silicon life:

A far greater number of silicon compounds is insoluble in water than carbon compounds. For all these reasons, silicon life could not be expected to develop beyond comparatively low and primitive stages, perhaps only plant life. Earth plant life is based on PHOTOSYNTHESIS, a process of making glucose sugar—the basic plant food —out of water, carbon dioxide (CO_2) and the energy of sunlight.

In a silicon world a similar process would be incomparably more difficult. First of all, silicon dioxide (SiO_2) is not a gas as is carbon dioxide, but a solid substance. Therefore, it would be carried to the silicon plant only in liquid form, as a silicic acid or as an extremely fine powder, carried by the atmospheric gases (as an aerosol). Because of the high chemical affinity of silicon to oxygen, much more energy is required to separate the two than to separate carbon and oxygen. The sunlight would therefore have to come from a star of much higher radiation intensity than the sun, so high that it would kill Earth life instantaneously. This also means that the surface temperature in the silicon world would be unbearable for man. This requirement is, of course, not compatible with the assumption that liquids can exist on its surface, unless it is a giant planet much larger than Earth whose gravitational pull is strong enough to hold an enormous atmosphere whose pressure on the surface would prevent the liquid from boiling away. Such atmosphere is unlikely to be transparent to the light of its sun, thereby rendering silicon-photosynthesis impossible in the first place. Thus inconsistencies arise at every turn.

But suppose all this could somehow be resolved. Then, if it is assumed that the silicon dioxide is available in liquid form, there must be visualized a static (plant) life which can be simultaneously exposed to sunlight and to silicic acid. A somewhat greater degree of freedom of growth could be attained if the SiO_2 were available in the form of aerosols. What about mobile ("animal") life? On Earth plant life "inhales" atmospheric CO_2 and "exhales" excess oxygen (O_2) produced through photosynthesis. Animals inhale O_2 and exhale CO_2. Plants and animals are fully complementary.

In a silicon world plants must inhale SiO_2 and exhale O_2 and animals must inhale O_2 and exhale SiO_2, a difficult process if one considers that SiO_2 is a solid. Somehow the animal would have to replace the silicon lost by exhaling. It would take a stomach of astounding capabilities to digest silicon plants. Also, whatever silico hydrates the "silicon blood" of this animal contains must be carefully protected from destruction by the inhaled oxygen. It is a fantastic aspect to consider that the very gas the animal needs to live is at the same time a terribly destructive potential poison.

Imagine a giant planet near a blue-white star showering the planet with enormous quantities of radiation energy, a huge but transparent atmosphere, misty from thinly distributed SiO_2 aerosols and a soil somehow "moist" with silicic acid. Plants rigid with heavy silicon shells squat on the ground. Animals, not gracious or tall or fast, but crawling creatures of the shape of a platypus, short flat worms, encrusted in heavy silicon armor would move slowly about, "eating" plants or each other with nutcracker-like jaws. They would breathe somehow with great difficulty and exhale a stream of gray-white silicon dioxide powder. Their excrements would resemble splintered glass. An impossible world? Not necessarily. Too little is known about the wonders of life in the universe to make such a presumptuous statement. It appears more certain, however, that this is an unlikely world, inferior to a carbon life world and much more rare.   K. A. E.
SEE ALSO: CARBON LIFE

Silicone (SIL–ih–kohn) Silicones are new, man-made compounds. Chemists have made silicones in solid, liquid, and gaseous forms. Some silicones act like rubber, but resist heat better. Others are used as lubricants.

The main chemical parts (or molecular radicals) of silicones are long chains of oxygen and silicon atoms. Various atomic groups of HYDROCARBONS, when chemically combined with these radicals, form the various silicones. They have some of the properties of organic materials such as rubber and oil, and also of inorganic materials such as sand and glass.   D. A. B.

Silk see Silkworm
Silk-cotton tree see Kapok

The female silkworm moth lays 300 to 400 eggs

✳ THINGS TO DO

RAISING YOUR OWN SILK

1   Eggs of the silkworm moth are difficult to find in nature. Most biological supply houses will furnish them. Put the eggs in a glass covered carton and keep them at room temperature out of direct sunlight.

2   After a few days small black larvae will appear. Feed them fresh, dry mulberry or osage-orange leaves each day.

3   In about five weeks put a stick in the box. The larvae will crawl on to it and spin their cocoons.

4   Drop the cocoon into boiling water for three minutes to kill the pupa. With great care unravel the silk fiber. A single fiber may measure three thousand yards.

Silkworm The silkworm is really not a worm at all. It is the caterpillar, or larva, of the silkworm moth. It uses the silk it makes to spin the cocoon necessary for it to become an adult.

Silkworms are raised by silk farmers, especially in Japan, China and France. The female silkworm moth lays between 300 to 400 eggs at a time on special pieces of paper. The eggs hatch into small, white silkworms, the larvae. They are fed chopped mulberry leaves, the only food they will eat. After eating, growing and molting for about four or five weeks, the larvae are ready to spin the all-important cocoons.

The silk of the silkworm is stored in two sacs, one along each side of its body. These sacs are connected by tubes to an opening below the mouth called the *spinneret*. When the liquid silk comes out of the silkworm's body, it becomes hard. It comes out as one long thread, and the silkworm fastens one end to a twig or straw on the tray where it spins its cocoon. Then it winds the silk around its body to make a cocoon that looks like a peanut shell when it is finished. The silkworm is not allowed to develop into a moth if its cocoon is to be used to make silk.

A silkworm larva grows from $\frac{1}{8}$ inch when it hatches from the egg to three inches when it is full grown. It has three pairs of true legs and five pairs of leg-like bits of flesh. The COCOON, which takes about three days to be spun, is made of one continuous silk filament 800 to 1200 yards long and may vary from white to golden yellow in color. If the silkworm is undisturbed, it will turn into a pupa and bore its way out in two or three weeks by excreting an alkaline liquid, dissolving the filament. Most cocoons, however, will be unwound for their unbroken silk fibers. The pupae inside are killed before they emerge by oven or steam-heating the whole unopened cocoons.

Some larvae, of course, are allowed to develop into pupae and then MOTHS so that eggs will be laid. The adult moth is a large white moth with black-lined wings. It cannot eat, its wings are too weak for it to fly, and it lives for only a few days.   H. J. C.

SEE ALSO: METAMORPHOSIS, MOLTING

Silt see Ocean, River

Silver is one of the precious metals

Buchsbaum

The silverfish is a household pest

Silver Silver is a precious metal that costs about 1/30 the price of gold. Pure silver has a brilliant white luster. Its alloys such as *sterling* (with copper) have warmer tints. Silver does not react with oxygen or vegetable and mineral acids, so it is used in the finer food utensils. However, it does combine with sulfur compounds in foods and polluted air, forming black silver sulfide. This is called *tarnish*.

Silver is found in various forms of ores. The processing of it is quite complex. Great deposits of native, or uncombined, silver were found in the western states. The commonest ore is a compound of silver and sulfur. Other ores contain combinations of silver with antimony, chlorine, and lead, as well as with gold, mercury, and copper.

Silver is too soft to be used in a pure state. It is usually alloyed with other metals. *Sterling silver* contains at least 925 parts silver and 75 parts copper. In England, coins are sterling. In the United States, coins are 900 parts silver and 100 parts copper.

Silver is best known for its use in tableware, ornaments, and coinage. Silver is often plated in a thin layer onto cheaper base metals. For certain purposes, this plating is very satisfactory, though the plate may wear off with use. The beauty of silver makes it desirable for many purposes. Its malleability and ductility (ability to be hammered and drawn) allow it to be easily and beautifully worked for all kinds of ornaments. (Sheets can be made so thin that a stack of 100,000 will only be an inch thick.) In compounds silver is used in photography and in making mirrors. Amalgams of silver with mercury are used in dentistry for fillings.

Of all metals, silver is the best conductor of electricity, and, next to gold, of heat.

Silver (symbol Ag from Latin *argentum*) has atomic number 47. Its atomic weight is 107.870 (107.880, O = 16). D. J. I.

SEE ALSO: ATOM, ELEMENTS, METAL

Silverfish Silverfish are wingless insects about one-half inch long. They have long feelers and abdomens of ten or eleven segments. They are also called *Bristletails*. They are household pests because they will eat any paper with glue on it and starch in clothes.

Extending from the abdomen is a segmented tail and several pairs of jointed bristles (*cerci*). Their bodies have silvery scales. METAMORPHOSIS is *gradual* as in GRASSHOPPERS. Unlike grasshoppers, silverfish molt after they reach sexual maturity. These insects are primitive and belong in the order Thysanura. J. C. K.

SEE ALSO: INSECTA

Simmond's disease A small organ called the *pituitary gland* lies under the middle of the brain. This gland is the master gland that controls all the other glands in the body. There are two parts of the pituitary gland. When the front part is destroyed, the other glands fail to work. This causes Simmond's disease.

The anterior lobe of the pituitary gland secretes HORMONES that stimulate the thyroid, adrenal, and sex glands. These glands, in turn, secrete their own hormones. All, working together, produce normal growth and development. When the balance is destroyed by the destruction of the pituitary (by tumor or more frequently by a blood clot), the obvious effect is great weight loss and wasting away of body tissues. By far, the most frequent cause of this condition is a difficult pregnancy with hemorrhage and SHOCK. Fortunately, the condition is rare. Treatment of Simmond's disease consists of supplying the missing hormones.

A condition similar to Simmond's disease in symptoms is *anorexia nervosa*. This, however, is a psychiatric disorder and does not involve the pituitary gland. B. M. H.

SEE ALSO: ENDOCRINE GLANDS, PITUITARY GLANDS

Simple machines see Machines, simple

Sinanthropus see Evolution of man

Sinkhole A sinkhole is an opening in the ground commonly found in regions of *limestone deposits*. These deposits occur where ancient warm seas once covered the land.

These ancient seas were shallow and supported abundant plant and animal life. The marine animal life was responsible for the limestone deposits. As these animals died, their remains filtered to the bottom of the sea and accumulated in great amounts. The skeletal remains of these animals contained a large amount of the mineral *calcite*. After the sea retreated, these accumulations were covered by other deposits and became the limestone layers found today.

Ground water later dissolved away portions of these deposits. This occurred because carbon dioxide dissolved in water, such as rain, forms the weak acid *carbonic acid*. When the earth's water contains this acid in both surface and sub-surface, it will dissolve limestone which is primarily calcium carbonate and soluble in acids. As the water solution proceeds, caverns are formed. These caverns, such as the *Mammoth Cave* of Kentucky, may remain as hollows beneath the earth. Sometimes however, cave-ins occur. These breaks through the roof of a subterranean cavern are called sinkholes. They may provide entry for *spelunkers* (cave explorers) or they may flood and form ponds or lakes.   D. J. I.

SEE ALSO: CAVE, GEOLOGY

Sinkholes are found in areas of underground limestone deposits

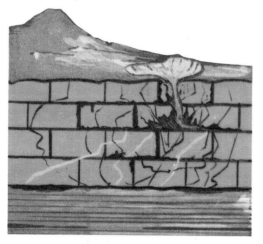

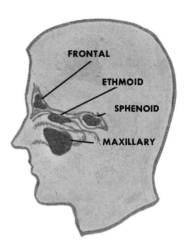

Location of sinuses

Sinus (SY-nuss) A sinus is a hollow cavity or channel in an organ, bone, tissue or similar body part. Usually the word *sinus* refers to one of the four pairs of cavities in the face bones of man. These areas connect with and drain fluid into the inside of the nose through small openings.

The *frontal* pair is located above and behind the eyebrows Their size varies with different people. The *maxillaries* are largest and are to the side of the nose and beneath the eyes. The chambered *ethmoids* lie behind the lateral bone of the nose. The *sphenoids* are found on the upper back part of the nasal cavity.

A sinus is lined with columnar cells bearing small hairs or *cilia* which move the fluid toward the nasal opening. Glands embedded in the tissue secrete mucous.

There is no satisfactory explanation of the functions of the sinuses. They may help to warm and moisten the air one breathes in because of their direct connection with the pharynx. Bacteria and other foreign material is trapped in the mucous and propelled to the throat. And the hollow chambers no doubt affect the sound of the voice and the contours of the face.

Inflammation of the sinus membranes produces a disorder called *sinusitis*. Several respiratory disorders cause the membrane to produce abundant mucous which cannot drain. The resulting pressure causes physical distress.   H. J. C.

Siphon (SYE-fun) A siphon is any tube-like device which carries liquids higher than their own level and then empties them at a lower level. Atmospheric pressure is usually great enough to keep the tubing filled with the LIQUID.

No gases can be present in the tube, and as long as there is a supply of liquid at the upper level, the siphon will continue to flow. GRAVITY has more liquid on which to pull on the one side of the tubing, tipping the balance to cause the motion.

A water siphon works up to about 34 feet at sea level. Mercury would siphon up to about 32 inches. F. R. W.

Sirius (SIR-ee-us) Sirius is the brightest star in the sky as seen from earth. It is a blue-white star about nine light-years away from earth. Only the sun, moon, Venus, and Jupiter are of greater magnitude.

Sirius is called the *Dog Star*. It is located in the constellation of *Canis Major*, the Great Dog. On star maps, it is the star that represents the nose of the dog. It rises soon after and slightly south of *Orion*. Sirius can be viewed during the summer in the Southern Hemisphere and during the winter in the Northern Hemisphere. H. S. G.
SEE ALSO: CANIS MAJOR AND MINOR, STARS

Sisal (SYE-suhl) Sisal is an agave plant that grows in Central America, the East and West Indies, Florida, Mexico, Hawaii, and parts of Africa. Sisal thrives in arid, rocky places. The fiber of this plant is sisal HEMP, used in making ropes, twine, and lariats.

The agave fibers rank next to cotton in commercial importance. The agaves are stemless perennials with long, pointed, fleshy leaves rising from the base at the ground. These leaves contain the fibers, which are removed by hand or machine. The leaves may be from two to five feet in length. The numerous species are very drought resistant and well adapted to dry sterile soils. They will grow where all other plants fail.

Sisal is the fiber which is scraped out from the leaf tissue. It is straw-colored, hard, wiry, and elastic. A species native to Mexico and Central America, it is now cultivated in Hawaii, the East and West Indies, and many sections of Africa. M. R. L.

Skate Skates are flat, triangular-shaped fish that live in the sea. They are related to SHARKS and RAYS. Some live in very deep water. Skates are found in most cool seas of the world.

Their pectoral fins, which are expanded and resemble wings, are used for locomotion. They wave these winglike fins up and down to propel themselves forward. A skate's long, thin tail has two small fins on it, and it is used as a steering device. Skates may be up to eight feet long and from a foot to twenty feet across including their winglike fins. Their eyes are close together on top of the head, while the mouth and gill slits are underneath. They have many rows of small, rounded teeth.

Skates have cartilage or gristle rather than true bone in their skeletons, and they lack true gill covers. They are covered with spiny scales known as *placoid scales*. Skates use spiracles (two-valved openings behind the eyes) to take in water. Water enters the spiracles and passes out through the gill slits. This arrangement makes it possible for the skate to lie on the ocean floor and inhale without taking in debris.

Skates have internal fertilization. The females, which are larger than the males, lay flat, rectangular eggs in cases of horn (keratin). Tendrils that extend from the corners of these cases hook onto vegetation. Incubation time varies from four and one half to fifteen months. J. C. K.
SEE ALSO: RAY, SHARK

Skeletal joints see Joints, skeletal

The skate's fins resemble wings

Skeleton The skeletal system gives support, shape, and protection to the body of an animal. Some skeletons are on the outside of the body, as in insects (*exoskeletons*). Others are on the inside, as in man (*endoskeletons*). Exoskeletons are often made of limestone, silica, or chitin. Endoskeletons are made of lime (as in bone) or of cartilage. They are harder and more rigid than exoskeletons.

COELENTERATES

Coelenterates have three types of skeletons. In hydra, support is furnished by the *mesoglea*. Mesoglea is a jelly-like, noncellular substance between the inner and outer cellular layers of the body wall.

Obelia, a colonial coelenterate, has a chitinous, horny *perisarc* covering the stems of the colony. The perisarc, an exoskeleton, both protects and supports.

Coral polyps (individuals) secrete limestone cups for protection and support. If the coral is a colonial type, the many limestone cups together may form a huge limestone mass known as a coral reef.

PROTOZOA

Some of the Protozoa have protective exoskeletons. Foraminifera, related to the ameba, secrete shells made of silica or lime. Small holes all over the shells allow for the extension of pseudopodia.

PLATYHELMINTHES,

NEMATHELMINTHES, AND ANNELIDS

These groups, flatworms, the roundworms, and segmented worms secrete a CUTICLE for body protection. They do not have skeletons.

ARTHROPODA

The exoskeleton of such arthropods as the crayfish and insect is secreted by the epidermis (hypodermis). Body muscles are connected to it, and it serves for protection. In order to allow for growth, it is softened, shed and formed anew. For the most part,

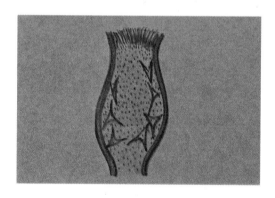

SPONGES (PORIFERA)

There are several kinds of skeletons among the sponges. The skeletons are usually composed of variously shaped spicules. SPICULES are made of lime or silica. Sponges like the common bath sponge have a skeleton of a protein-like fibrous material called *spongin*. Spongin is arranged in a branching network which supports the soft protoplasmic cells of the sponge.

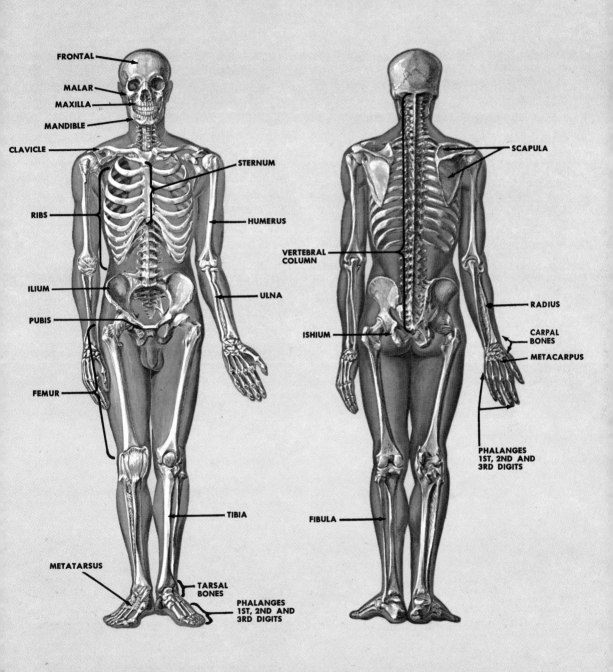

FRONTAL

MALAR

MAXILLA

MANDIBLE

CLAVICLE

STERNUM

RIBS

HUMERUS

ILIUM

ULNA

PUBIS

FEMUR

TIBIA

METATARSUS

TARSAL BONES

PHALANGES 1ST, 2ND AND 3RD DIGITS

SCAPULA

VERTEBRAL COLUMN

ISHIUM

RADIUS

CARPAL BONES

METACARPUS

PHALANGES 1ST, 2ND AND 3RD DIGITS

FIBULA

©Denoyer-Geppert Co.

this cuticle is composed of a protein called *arthropodin* and a carbohydrate called CHITIN. It is made of three layers. Among various arthropods, and also in different areas of the body, this cuticle is changed for different purposes. Between segments it is soft and pliable to allow for movement. It has been found that the cuticle is harder in crayfish than in many insects, because in crayfish it contains lime.

MOLLUSCA

The soft body of a mollusk (snails, clams, oysters) is wrapped with a fleshy covering called a *mantle*. Usually a well developed shell made of carbonate of lime is secreted by the mantle. It serves for protection and muscle attachment. Slugs, related to snails, either have no shell or a very small one. Another mollusk, chiton, has a series of external plates connected by parts of the mantle. Snails have coiled, one-piece shells, while those of clams and oysters are two pieces hinged together.

ECHINODERMATA

Echinoderms (starfish, sea urchins, sand dollars) have endoskeletons formed in the embryo from the same germ layer (meso-

Cross-section of starfish arm: A—movable section (spine), B—immovable section

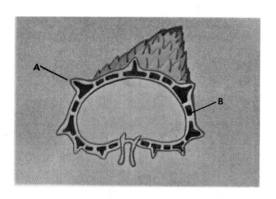

derm) as the vertebrate skeleton. The skeleton of echinoderms consists of *calcarious ossicles,* or plates, beneath the epidermis. There are also spines. Sea cucumbers have leathery skins without spines. Calcarious plates embedded in the skin are microscopic in size. Sea urchins have long, movable spines and a compact skeleton (the ossicles are close together.) Ossicles are present on the stalk of sea lilies, but spines are absent. Starfish have immovable spines and ossicles arranged in a definite pattern.

LOWER CHORDATES

Lower chordates have a supportive rod known as a *notochord*. In one group the notochord runs the length of the body, in another it is found only in the head region, while in a third group it occurs in the free-swimming larvae but not in the attached (sessile) adults.

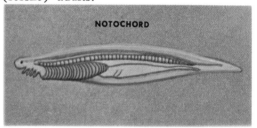

Amphioxus

VERTEBRATES

In higher chordates, the vertebrates, the notochord appears in the embryos, but in the adults it is usually replaced by a bony, or cartilaginous, endoskeleton. Body muscles are connected to the skeleton by tendons. The vertebrate endoskeleton is made up of a column of vertebrae enclosing the spinal cord, the cranium or brain case, two girdles for the attachment of appendages (arms, legs, fins, or wings) and two pairs of jointed appendages. Hair, feathers, scales, and fingernails may be traces of an exoskeleton.

The lampreys, the lowest class of vertebrates, lack paired fins, and have a notochord in the adult. There is more cartilage than bone in their skeletons.

Sharks have a skeleton made entirely of cartilage, paired fins, and, in the adult, a notochord.

Fish, amphibia (frogs and toads), reptiles, birds, and mammals have bony skeletons with vertebrae, crania, and girdles. Paired, jointed appendages are present except in snakes and one small group of amphibians. The notochord is absent in the adult.

THE SKELETON OF MAN

Man has the same skeletal plan as other vertebrates. The human skeleton is made of about two hundred bones. The long bones of the arms and legs contain marrow in which red blood cells are formed. Bones are connected at joints. Ball-and-socket joints occur where the arms and legs attach to the girdles to allow free movement. Hinged joints at the knees permit movement only in one direction. Pivot joints occur in the ankles and wrists, while the joints between the skull bones are not movable. At the joints, the ends of bones are covered with smooth cartilage and held together by several fibrous ligaments.

The skull, backbone, breastbone, and ribs are usually grouped and called the *axial skeleton*. There are 33 vertebrae, varying in size and shape, in the backbone. Twelve pair of ribs are connected to vertebrae. Ten pairs are attached in front to the breastbone (*sternum*). Two pairs (floating ribs) are unattached to the breastbone.

Leg and arm bones, plus the girdles which attach them to the axial skeleton, make up the *appendicular skeleton*.

The *pelvic girdle* to which legs are attached at the hip socket (acetabulum) consists of three fused bones (ilium, ischium, pubis). A leg is composed of a thigh bone (femur), a patella covering the knee, two long bones below the knee (tibia and fibula), seven ankle bones (tarsals), five bones in the instep of the foot (metatarsals), and fourteen bones in the toes (phalanges).

Arms are attached to the *pectoral girdle*. It is composed of two collarbones (clavicles) and two shoulder blades (scapulae). Hand bones are similar in number to foot bones. In the arm there is one humerus, two long bones below the elbow (radius and ulna), eight wrist bones (carpals), five bones in the hand (metacarpals), and fourteen bones in the fingers (phalanges.)   L. M.

SEE ALSO: ANIMALS, CLASSIFICATION OF; BONE; CHORDATA; HISTOLOGY; JOINTS, SKELETAL

✳ THINGS TO DO

CLEANING AND ASSEMBLING A SKELETON

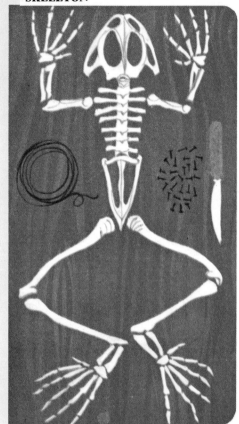

1   Cleaning and assembling a skeleton from each class of vertebrates is an enterprising task for the young scientist. He can use a fish, a frog, turt le, chicken, and a rodent for representative examples.

2   First remove the epidermal covering by skinning the animal. Boil it for half an hour. Cut, pick, and scrap all muscles and organs from the skeleton.

3   If necessary soak the bones in a caustic soda solution to remove any remaining tissue. Be careful!

4   To remove the grease from the skeleton soak it outdoors in a carbon tetrachloride solution for at least a day.

5   The final process of cleaning involves putting the bones in any household bleach to make them white.

6   Using wire and small screws reassemble the skeleton into the shape of the original animal. Mount it on a wooden base for support.

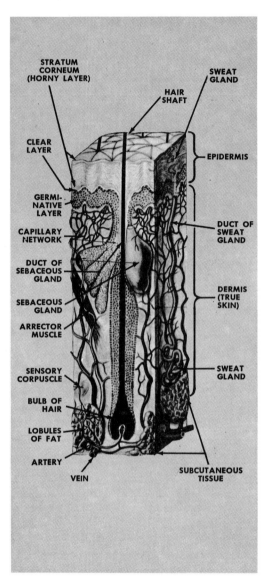

TODAY'S HEALTH, published by AMERICAN MEDICAL ASSOCIATION

Skin Skin is the covering for the body. In man and other land animals with backbones, the skin is made of layers of flattened cells with the outer layers dry or somewhat hardened and waterproof. Skin sometimes is changed, or modified into hair, nails, feathers, or some sort of shell for defense, or to keep animals warm or cool. The skin helps the body keep its proper temperature by the evaporation of perspiration, and by controlling the amount of blood near the surface. The skin also helps the body rid itself of wastes. Sensations such as touch, pain, heat, and cold are received by the nerves through the skin.

There are two main layers of the skin. The outer layer is called the *epidermis,* and the inner layer is called the *dermis, corium,* or *cutis.* The epidermis consists of several layers of which the first, or outermost, is the *stratum corneum,* or horny layer. It is made of many closely packed, dead, cornified, greatly flattened cells. These are continuously being cast off from the surface and replaced from lower layers.

The second layer of the epidermis is the *stratum lucidum,* which consists of several layers of closely packed scale-like cells. Next is the third layer, the *stratum granulosum,* the cells of which are not so flattened, and contain a substance called *keratohyaline.* Nails are considered modifications of this layer. The next layer is the *stratum germinativum,* which has from one to four layers of diamond-shaped cells with spine-like projections between the cells. The pigment in dark-skinned races is found in this layer. The deepest cells of this layer are columnar or cuboidal in shape. They divide to replace those lost in the outer layers.

The dermis, or corium, is a network of dense and interlacing fibers of connective tissue. Nerve endings, glands, hair follicles, and a rich supply of blood vessels are located here. The dermis has a papillary layer next to the epidermis with projections which fit up into corresponding places in the epidermis above. Sometimes these projections are so pronounced that the skin is ridged, as in the lines of fingerprints. In the deeper layer of the dermis the fibrous network is looser; fat globules are found here. Hair follicles also originate in this deeper layer. There is a network of blood vessels and nerves, and in some places, of muscle fibers.

In man, striated muscle fibers (under voluntary control) are found in the skin of the face and neck, and enable him to register facial expressions. These muscle fibers extend from the tissues (*subcutaneous*) below the skin into the lower layers of the dermis of the skin. Smooth muscles (not under voluntary control) are distributed around the hair follicles and glands. Their contraction causes "goose flesh" and "hair to stand on end."

Nerve fibrils go to the hair follicles, the sweat glands, and the muscular walls of the blood vessels. There are also free nerve endings and nerve-end organs, some of which receive sensations of heat, of cold, some pressure, and some pain. The distribution of the various kinds of nerve-end organs varies over the body. Sometimes the reception of one kind of sensation may be lost while others remain. For example, when a limb "goes to sleep," the sensation of cold is nearly lost but that of heat remains.

The glands in the skin are sweat glands and oil, or *sebaceous,* glands. Oil glands are usually found in the dermis where there are hairs, and their ducts open into the superficial parts of the hair follicle. There are two kinds of sweat glands. Those with simple tubular structure are found over the entire skin. Others with a branched complex structure are found only in the skin over arm pits, in the ear where specialized ones produce ear wax, and on the eyelids. E. M. S.

SEE ALSO: CONNECTIVE TISSUE, HAIR, NAILS, SKIN MODIFICATION, SWEAT GLAND

✳ **THINGS TO DO**

HOW DOES SKIN PROTECT YOU?

1 You will need pairs of fruit and vegetables the same size for this experiment: two carrots, two potatoes, two oranges, etc.

2 Remove the skin or peel from one of each pair. Let them stand exposed to the air for one week.

3 What happened to the peeled specimen in color and weight? Why?

TODAY'S HEALTH, published by AMERICAN MEDICAL ASSOCIATION

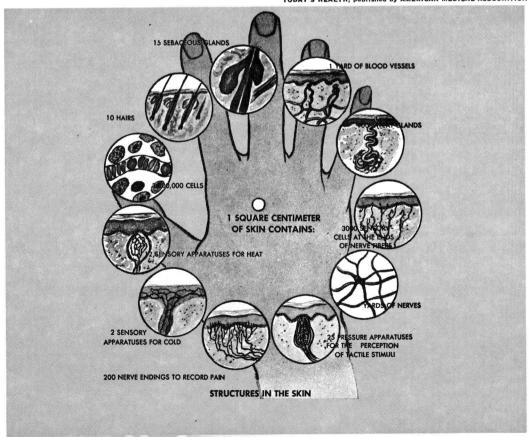

STRUCTURES IN THE SKIN

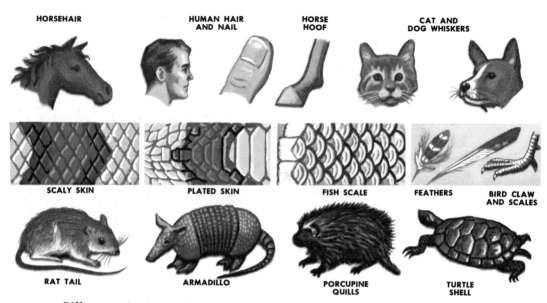

HORSEHAIR HUMAN HAIR AND NAIL HORSE HOOF CAT AND DOG WHISKERS

SCALY SKIN PLATED SKIN FISH SCALE FEATHERS BIRD CLAW AND SCALES

RAT TAIL ARMADILLO PORCUPINE QUILLS TURTLE SHELL

Different animals may have skin that has been modified for special functions

Skin modification The skin covering the body is sometimes changed in appearance and structure to protect animals in special ways from weather and enemies. Some of these modifications found in animals are hair, nails, scales, and feathers.

Snakes, lizards, and other reptiles have *dermal scales* which are shed by molting to allow for growth. Dermal scales grow out from the underlying layers of the skin. The feathers of birds are nonliving, cornified products of the skin. The hair-covering of still other animals varies in length, thickness, and texture, often with heavy underfur for body insulation and fewer longer guard hairs. Each hair usually grows to a definite length and stops; but the mane and tail of horses, and the hair on man's head, grow continuously. Specialized hairs are the quills on porcupines and the *vibrissae,* or long whiskers, around the mouth and nose of meat eaters (cats and dogs). Each vibrissa is surrounded at the base by nerve fibers, and receives touch sensations.

Other examples of skin modifications are spurs on bird legs; scales on the tails of muskrat, beaver, mouse and rat; and the hair-covered, armor-like bony epidermis of the armadillo. Beaks and leg coverings on birds and outer *scutes* (horny plates) on turtle shells are other examples.

Callouses form on palms and feet, and the skin of foot pads forms a cornified coating for protection against wear. Nails, horns, and hoofs, like other skin modifications, grow continuously from the base. Horns of cattle, sheep, and Old World antelope are cornified skin supported by a bony core. Deer antlers are not modified skin. *Baleen* (whalebone) and rhinoceros horns are made of epidermal hairy fibers cemented together and growing from dermal papillae rather than from hair follicles. Baleen, found in the mouths of whalebone whales, is a series of flattened triangular horny plates arranged on either side of the palate, with the inner edges frayed into fibers which act as strainers.

The cornified materials in skin modifications are keratins which are insoluble proteins. E. M. S.

SEE ALSO: FEATHER, HAIR, HISTOLOGY, HORN, HOOF, HYPERTROPHY, NAIL, SCALE, SKIN

Skin test A skin test is a scratch made on the skin, usually to diagnose an ALLERGY, by applying pollen to the scratch. Tuberculosis tests are also given on the skin.

Skin-diving see Oceanography

Skink see Lizard

Skull see Skeleton

The skunk is known for its strong odor

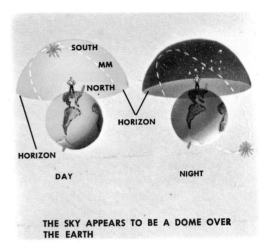
THE SKY APPEARS TO BE A DOME OVER THE EARTH

Skunk The skunk is a mammal about the size of a house cat. Skunks are sometimes called "wood pussies." Their best known characteristic is a strong, very unpleasant odor produced by a special fluid they release.

Skunks are found over most parts of the United States. Best known varieties are the striped skunk and the smaller spotted skunk. The striped skunk is most common. It has a long, black, bushy tail, thick glossy fur, and a white patch on its forehead.

Skunks eat grubs, eggs, poultry, small reptiles, and rodents. They prowl at night. No animal annoys the skunk. It is capable of spraying its yellowish fluid as far as ten feet. The fluid comes from two scent glands beneath the tail. The skunk uses this device only when frightened or provoked and, if necessary, discharges the fluid in a series of sprays. The fluid can burn skin and can be harmful to the eyes. Because of the skunk's unique method of defense, it is not often molested and leads a very independent, slow-moving life. Young skunks are playful and make good pets if the scent glands are removed. At times, skunk fur for coats has been popular. Otherwise the animal has little value to man.

During northern winters, skunks become drowsy but are not true hibernators. Following birth, young skunks live together through the winter. The following spring, they separate and find mates, living in tree trunks, burrows, or beneath houses. Skunks are related to the European polecat and belong to the WEASEL family. D. J. I.

Skunk cabbage see Wild flowers

Sky The sky appears to be a dome that extends from the observer's horizon to all points overhead. The atmosphere surrounding the earth makes the sky bright blue on clear days. Without the atmosphere which scatters the light waves coming from the sun, the sky would appear black, and the sun would be a bright spot in a black background.

The gases of the atmosphere act as a prism; they separate the colors of sunlight into the color spectrum. The atmosphere contains billions of microscopic dust particles, termed *condensation nuclei,* that interfere with the passage of light rays. The prism action of the atmosphere and what is referred to as "selective scattering" make the daytime sky look blue. Blue light is seen in the eye of the observer.

However, the dust particles interfere more with the passage of blue waves than they do with the passage of the longer yellow and red waves. When we look at the sun, it appears yellow because most of the blue light has been screened out by the dust particles. The nearer the sun is to the horizon, the more atmosphere its light must pass through. This makes the sun appear more red than yellow. Looking away from the sun to another part of the sky dome, the observer's eye receives most of the blue light waves that have been scattered out of the white light of the sun. This part of the sky appears blue. Clouds and water vapor also affect sky color. H. S. G.
SEE ALSO: ATMOSPHERE, EARTH, SPECTRUM, TNYDALL EFFECT

Skylark see Lark

Slag Slag is material remaining from ore-smelting processes in industry. It is usually grayish in color, and is commonly used in cinder roads. It is not strong enough for road surfaces where travel is heavy. Cinders are economical for paths or drives about houses where traffic is light.

There are various kinds of slag. One kind, which is a side product from steel blast furnaces, contains calcium, magnesium and aluminum silicates. Other slags contain iron silicates, lime, and other minerals. Some slag is re-processed to obtain these small remaining amounts of usable minerals.

Slag has come into use as a building material. It is mixed with concrete, and cast into blocks used in building. Cinder blocks are preferred to brick and concrete blocks because they are lighter in weight, and thus easier to transport and handle. They are strong and as fireproof as the other types. Because they have a rougher texture than bricks, however, they are not as desirable for use in exposed walls.   D. J. I.
SEE ALSO: STEEL

Slaked lime see Solvay process

Slate see Rocks

Sleep Sleep is a state during which body processes slow down. This allows the body to rest and repair itself. All animals need these rest periods, but true sleep occurs only in animals with highly organized NERVOUS SYSTEMS.

In most animals, periods of rest and activity alternate rhythmically. The ordinary earthworm has four rest periods each twenty-four hours. Such periods are probably not "brain" controlled since, when a worm is cut in half, each half shows the same rhythmical pattern. The largest ganglion, the "brain," does not seem to be necessary. In mammals, the brain appears to control sleep. When the spinal cord is cut, only the half of the body including the brain shows periods of rest and activity.

Aquatic mammals usually sleep on the surface of the water. The sea otter wraps its body in long pieces of kelp so that it does not drift while sleeping. In herds of resting mammals, some sleep while others stand guard.

Physiological changes accompany sleep in higher forms of life. Blood pressure and pulse rate decrease, and blood vessels in the skin dilate. Muscle tone, the state of partial contraction that healthy muscles exhibit, diminishes during sleep. Body functioning, or *metabolic rate,* decreases 10 to 15 percent below the basal rate (measured when the body is resting and not digesting a meal). Body temperature may drop to 97.8° or 98°F. It is believed that the sleep center is in the HYPOTHALAMUS of the brain. J. C. K.
SEE ALSO: HIBERNATION, METABOLISM, NOCTURNAL HABITS

Sleeping sickness "Sleeping sickness" is a name given to several kinds of illnesses accompanied by a drowsiness that progresses to a coma and frequently to death. There is much of this dangerous illness in Africa.

The most common variety is an illness called *African sleeping sickness.* It is caused by a protozoan parasite living in the blood of cattle and wild animals. The animals themselves show no sign of disease. When a certain type of fly, called the *tsetse fly*, bites an infected animal, it sucks the blood with the parasite into its stomach. If a tsetse fly bites a human, the parasites are allowed to enter the body where they invade the nervous system and cause inflammation around the brain.

In this country, a different kind of sleeping sickness is caused by a VIRUS. The St. Louis type appears in EPIDEMICS. The disease is spread by the bite of the mosquito, *Aedes egypti.* The virus multiplies after it gets into the body and produces inflammation of the brain (*encephalitis*).   B. M. H.

Sleet see Precipitation

Slide rule A slide rule is a mechanical instrument for doing mathematical problems more easily—mostly multiplication and division. It consists of movable pieces of wood containing *logarithmic* scales and matching *antilogarithms.*
SEE: COMPUTER

Sliding friction see Friction

Slime mold

Slime mold see Mold

Slip see Propagation

Sloth (SLAWTH) The sloth is a slow, clumsy animal that spends much time hanging upside down by all four feet from tree branches. It has sharp, long claws that curve. This feature is handy for hanging but slows the animal down when traveling on the ground. The sloth is about one and one-half feet long. Its fur is coarse and gray, blending into the scenery around it.

There are two genera of sloths. The *two-toed sloth* has two toes on the front feet but three on the back. The *three-toed sloth,* in addition to being different by having three toes, has nine cervical vertebrae which is unusual because most mammals have seven. This, plus the extra long trachea, enable the sloth to reach for its food without moving far from its upside down position.

Sloths belong to the order *Edentata,* along with ANTEATERS and ARMADILLOS. They inhabit the tropical forests of Central and South America. They eat leaves and young twigs of the cecropia tree. One variety of sloth lives symbiotically with ALGAE. The algae get closer to the light when carried to the tops of trees and the sloth is difficult to find when coated with this plant.

Fossils of the *ground sloth* were discovered in the recesses of a New Mexico cave. Calculations of its age were dated back to the Pleistocene times.   H. J. C.
SEE ALSO: MAMMALIA

Chicago Natural History Museum

Two-toed Choloepus sloth

Slug Slugs are snails with either very thin shells or none at all. One of the few members of the MOLLUSCA without

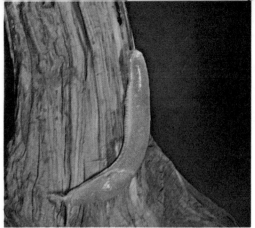
Buchsbaum

The slug is a mollusk

well-developed shells, their soft bodies are flat instead of coiled. The slug is wrapped in a mantle like other snails. It creeps along on a flat yellowish foot that secretes a mucus on which it slides. Slugs have two pairs of tentacles, or feelers, on their heads. Their eyes are located at the ends of the larger pair. Slugs range in size from one and one half to four inches long.

Common garden slugs are gray, yellow, or brown, spotted with black. They are slimy. These land forms are *herbivorous* and usually look for food at night. They can find their way by their sense of smell. One kind of slug eats into heads of lettuce and ruins them. In general, the plant-eating slugs have smaller and fewer teeth than the *carnivorous* slugs.

Some of the marine sea slugs are brightly colored. They are carnivorous. Like all members of the snail group, they have a rasping tongue called a *radula.* Teeth on the radula are arranged in rows and vary in number.

The female lays five hundred to eight hundred white eggs in damp soil.   P. G. B.
SEE ALSO: MOLLUSCA

Smallpox Smallpox is a severe, contagious disease caused by a VIRUS. Only vaccination prevents the disease.

Smallpox, or *variola,* is an ancient disease. It was known in China and India at least two thousand years ago. Rhazes, a Persian physician, was the first to accurately describe it.

In the eleventh century, the disease was carried from the East to Europe where, during the Middle Ages, a single epidemic killed almost one quarter of the people. Later, during the age of exploration, the Spaniards brought smallpox to Mexico. Thousands of

---

✳ **THINGS TO DO**

IS YOUR SENSE OF SMELL MORE PERCEPTIVE THAN YOUR SENSE OF TASTE?

Cut small cubes of raw potato, onion, apple, and pear. Take turns with a friend on this experiment and compare the results. The one being experimented upon should be blindfolded. Hold a piece of onion direct- ly under his nose and have him eat a piece of potato. Ask him which one he is eating. Repeat by smelling the pear and eating the apple. Which is more perceptive—the sense of smell or taste?

Mexican Indians died of the disease in 1520. The last epidemic in this country occurred in Detroit, Michigan, in 1924. There were 160 deaths. This country will never have another major smallpox epidemic because of strict vaccination requirements. However, the disease remains a major cause of death in heavily populated countries, such as China and India, where children are not vaccinated.

Smallpox spreads rapidly from person to person, as do the BLACK DEATH, or plague, and TYPHOID fever.

Smallpox has an abrupt onset about two weeks after a person has been exposed. Its symptoms include headache and pain in the lower back accompanied by fever, severe aching, and often vomiting. Early on the fourth day, a skin eruption appears on the face. The red marks rapidly become blisters and fill with pus. The rash spreads over the body down to the legs and feet. In nine days, the blisters dry and form scabs that eventually drop off. Severe cases may be complicated by secondary infection of sores or severe bleeding. Scars on the skin are likely to result because the infection penetrates the skin deeply.

A new medicine has been developed which is a treatment for smallpox. However, vaccination remains the best way to prevent the disease. If 80 percent of the world's population could be vaccinated, smallpox would disappear. The World Health Organization expects to accomplish this by 1978. B. M. H.

SEE ALSO: BLACK DEATH; JENNER, EDWARD; VACCINE

Smell Smell is one of the senses with which nature has provided many animals. It is used to search for food or to protect them from danger. Smell is a well-developed sense in many mammals, especially wild animals. Fishes and insects also have organs of smell. In man this sense is not as well developed.

Smell is called the *olfactory* sense. It comes into activity when molecules (gases) of certain substances enter the nose. In the upper part are special nerve endings. Liquid in the nasal passage dissolves the incoming gases, which react chemically on the olfactory nerve endings. These transmit nerve messages to the brain.

Smell is often a combination of reactions to odor, taste, temperature, pain, and even sight. When only the sense of smell reacts, a false or incomplete impression may be gained. Thus appreciation for a hamburger may be more intense if it is seen, felt, and tasted, as well as smelled.

After prolonged activity, olfactory nerves are insensitive, which explains why one may not notice the presence of a skunk after a period of being near it.

In vertebrates olfactory nerves are typically located in the nasal passages.

Odors may be classified into a few groups, such as aromatic, fragrant, or burnt. D. J. I.

SEE ALSO: NOSE, SENSE ORGANS

Smelling salts Smelling salts are used to revive a person from a fainting spell. They are composed of ammonium carbonate and fragrant oils.

Moist ammonium carbonate constantly gives off AMMONIA gas. When cautiously inhaled, ammonia stimulates the cells lining the nose, throat, and bronchial tubes. It causes the muscles of the breathing organ to work more quickly. It also shrinks stuffy nasal passages.

In order to reduce the sharpness of the ammonia odor, various perfume or essential oils are added. Menthol, eucalyptus oil, and lemon oil are the more common odor-masking substances. A solution of ammonia called "spirits of ammonia" is sometimes used for the same purpose as smelling salts.

M. S.

Smelt is a commercial food fish

Smelt True smelts are small inland fish that are often used as food fish. They were named from their characteristic odor. The cold waters of the Northern Hemisphere are their habitat. They have silvery sides, dark backs, and are about eight inches long. Their teeth are well developed. Some species have both marine and freshwater populations. For example, one species is marine in Japan and freshwater in California rivers. Some smelt, caught in the northern United States by ice fishing, are a freshwater population of an Atlantic smelt.

Smelts are very abundant where they occur. Since they serve as food for many larger fish, they are often near the base of a *food chain*. It is not unusual for sixty thousand smelt to be netted during a three-hour period. Often the fishing season corresponds to the SPAWNING period. Many tons of smelt are caught during the spring run of Pacific smelt into the Columbia River.

Another small silver fish is found with smelt and is often confused with them. These are in the Silversides family and are relatives of the BARRACUDAS and MULLETS. Unlike smelts they have silver bands on each side and a different fin structure.

J. C. K.

SEE ALSO: SPAWNING

Smilax see Wild flowers

Smog (SMAHG) Smog is a combination of smoke, various waste gases, dust, and fog. Smog most often occurs over large urban areas that have a large concentration of industry and automobile traffic. Smog can present a health hazard to the people living in these regions. It diminishes visibility and is a hindrance to air travel.

Smog is most likely to form during times when there is little or no convection taking place in the atmosphere. Smoke and chemical fumes combine with fog to form a dense cloud. If atmospheric conditions remain the same and there are no rising air currents to carry smog away, it may linger for days.

H. S. G.

Smoke Smoke is unburned carbon. When it accumulates in places like smoke pipes and chimneys, it is called *soot*.

Soft coal commonly used by steel mills, ships, and railroads is often not completely burned. As a result, large volumes of smoke pour out of smokestacks and chimneys, severely affecting the neighboring areas. Sunshine is blacked out, the air is contaminated, and it is impossible to keep clean.

Many communities have passed laws against smoke nuisance. The installation of smoke screens, better firing, and the use of hard coal is recommended and sometimes demanded.

V. V. N.

SEE ALSO: COAL

Smut see Corn, Plant diseases

Burning leaves create a fragrant smoke

Buchsbaum

Marine coast snails

Snail Snails comprise a large family of the *gastropod* group. They inhabit fresh and sea water, marshes, damp and shady garden areas, and trees. All snails, with the exception of the SLUG, wear a spiral shell and travel by means of a broad, muscular foot that extends from the shell. Moisture is important for them. To conserve moisture the snail retires within the shell and closes the opening with the flat foot, sealing the edges with a mucous-like secretion. This same secretion is used by the slug, which has no shell for protection, to lubricate and protect its tough body as it travels.

Below the shell of the snail the head and foot are joined together. The head bears retractable tentacles, the tips of which have eyes with cornea, lens, and retina. Probably there is also an organ for smell. Below the mouth is a pedal organ that secretes the slime track. The anus and respiratory pore are at the shell edge in the mantle margin. Sea mollusks have gills, fresh water snails have both gills and lungs, and land snails have lungs, a network of blood vessels in the mantle around the mantle cavity in the shell. Air enters and leaves by the respiratory pore.

A single kidney discharges into the mantle cavity and drains blood from the cavity around the heart. The heart has a single ventricle and auricle. The digestive system consists of the mouth, pharynx with a horny "jaw" and radula used for tearing off bits of food, a thin esophagus, a crop, stomach, coiled intestine, and anus. Salivary glands secrete through ducts into the pharynx, and the liver located high in the shell secretes into the stomach.

In some species, one animal has both the male and female organs. The genital pore is near the head.   E. M. S.

SEE ALSO: MOLLUSCA, PERIWINKLE

Snakeroot see Wild flowers

Snakes Snakes, like most other reptiles, have scales for body covering. Unlike most reptiles, they either lack legs or, as in the case of the boas, have mere remnants of legs.

Many snakes are non-poisonous. They usually lay rubbery-shelled eggs; but some kinds produce living young.

People often fear snakes for no reason except that they, unfortunately, have been taught that all snakes are harmful, poisonous, and slimy. Many people will kill snakes on sight; this is wrong, because many snakes are useful as destroyers of rodents and other pests.

Snakes vary in size from the tiny species a few inches long to giants over thirty feet in length. They have up to three hundred vertebrae. Their bodies are covered with scales that are smooth and dry: thus they are not slimy. The shed their skins at least once, but ordinarily several times, a year. Their eyes have permanent, transparent caps, and are always open.

Snakes have numerous teeth, which are sharp-pointed and aimed inward; thus they are not adapted for chewing like the teeth of many other animals but for drawing food into the throat and stomach.

Snakes are cold-blooded, that is, their bodies vary in temperature with the environment. They ordinarily die in cold a few degrees below freezing or in heat over 100° F. Thus snakes are rare in the arctic but abundant in temperate and tropical regions. In winter they hibernate beneath the ground.

Some species of snakes have hollow

✳ THINGS TO DO

KEEPING SNAKES AS PETS

1. An old aquarium or similar house will serve as a comfortable home for a pet snake. They do not like drafts. Wire cages are rough on their skin as they slide about. Be sure the cover is fastened securely.
2. Stock the house with plants fitting to the species: woodland, desert, or aquatic habitat (see TERRARIUM for stocking).
3. Snakes will need fresh water daily and raw meat, small rodents, or live worms weekly. If the pet fails to eat and behave normally after two weeks in captivity, return it to its natural environment.
4. When handling a snake hold it near the head and in the center of its body. Quick motions and the fear of falling will frighten them. Leave snakes alone at feeding time or while they are molting.

teeth (*fangs*) with which they can inject poison into prey and enemies. Most snakes eat insects and rodents. Some tropical species can consume pigs. They are adept at catching prey, but they are not as fast in crawling as many people think they are. They crawl by pushing each body-curve against projections on the ground. On a completely smooth surface, they writhe helplessly, making no forward progress.

In feeding, a snake often seizes its prey from a coiled, aiming position; then it

FACTS ABOUT IMPORTANT SNAKES

Common name (or group)	Location	Size — Average	Known record
Poisonous species:			
Adder (vague, common name) see cobra, puff adder, ringhals	United States and elsewhere		
Asp (kinds of cobras) Legend of Cleopatra's asp	Africa, Asia, Southern Europe	Variable up to 5 feet	
Bushmaster	Central and South America	7-8 feet	12 feet
Cobra (species of naja)	Asia and Africa	4-5 feet	(king) 18 ft. 4 in.
Copperhead ("moccasin")	North America	2-3 feet	4 ft. 6 in.
Coral (see mimic corals) Red and yellow stripe next to each other	Southern United States	2-2½ feet	4 feet
Cottonmouth (water moccasin)	Southern United States	2½-4 feet	6 ft. 2 in.
Diamondback rattler (two species)	North America	2½-6 feet	8 ft. (Eastern)
Fer de lance (pit viper)	Tropical America	5 ft. 7 in.	9 feet
Rattlesnake (thirty species, see Diamondback and sidewinder)	North America		
Sidewinder (rattlesnake)	Western U.S.A. and Mexico	2-3½ feet	
Ringhals, a spitting cobra (see non-poisonous ringneck)	South America	3-4 feet	
Viper, many species (see fer de lance)	Worldwide		
Non-poisonous species			
Anaconda	South America	20 feet	37 feet
Boa constrictor	South America	12-15 ft.	18½ feet
Black racer (black snake)	North America	3-5 feet	6 ft. 1 in.
Bull snake, several subspecies exist	United States	5 feet	8 ft. 2 in.
Chicken (yellow rat snake)	Eastern United States	3½-6 feet	7 feet
California boa, related to rubber boas	Mexico, Southwestern U.S.A.	approx. 2-2½ Ft.	
Garter snake, many subspecies exist	North America	1½-2 feet	(Eastern) 4 ft.
Green snakes (two United States species)	North America and Asia	2-2½ ft. (U.S.A.)	3½ ft.
King snakes (Lampropeltis) many species (see milk snake)	United States and Canada		
Milk snake (L. doliata), (a kind of king snake)	Eastern North America	2-3 feet	3 ft. 11¼ in.
Mimic coral snake. Red and yellow stripe is separated by black stripe	Worldwide	Variable sizes	
Mud snake (Farancia species)	Florida	3½-4½ feet	6 feet
Puff adder (hog-nosed snake) Hiss and spread like cobras	North central America	1½-2½ feet	3 ft. 8 in.
Python (several species) Asian python is reticulated in coloring	Southern Asia, Australia and Africa	25 ft. (African) 32 ft. (Asian)	
Ringneck (several species) Not to be confused with poisonous ringhal	North America	2-3½ feet	
Sand boas (Eryx species)	Asia and Africa	2-3 feet	
Whip snakes (Masticophis) Vibrates tail like rattlers	Americas	3½-5 feet	8 ft. 8 in. (Eastern)

Courtesy of Clifford H. Pope, Herpetologist

makes a sudden, forward jab of the head. All food is swallowed whole and unchewed. The digestive juices of a snake are strong enough to digest all parts except fur and feathers. A snake can swallow animals much greater in diameter than itself because it has a mouth that stretches, and lower jaws which fold outward at their hinges and separate temporarily at the front. Some kinds of snakes suffocate their prey first, using the pressure (constriction) of their coils. They do not really crush their prey to death by breaking bones and tissues.

Snakes "hear" vibrations from the ground through their concealed ears. They smell partly through the nose and partly by carrying bits of materials on the forked tongue to a sense organ in the roof of the mouth. The tongue also provides a keen sense of touch; it does not sting, and is very delicate.

Few people in the temperate regions suffer bites from poisonous snakes; but in some less urbanized tropical regions, such as rural India, injuries from snakes are more frequent.

Snakes ordinarily will avoid man, and almost never attack unless they are cornered, handled, or stepped on. They then react from fear.   D. J. I.

SEE ALSO: CHORDATA, REPTILIA

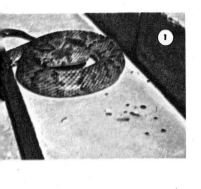

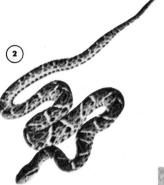

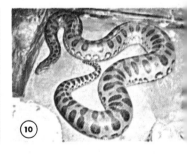

1—COTTONMOUTH
2—FER-DE-LANCE
3—EUROPEAN VIPER
4—HOG-NOSED SNAKE
5—DIAMONDBACK
   RATTLER
6—COACH WHIP
7—BULL SNAKE
8—INDIGO RACER
9—PRAIRIE RATTLER
10—ANACONDA
11—RAT SNAKE
12—COBRA
13—GARTER SNAKE

All pictures Courtesy Society For Visual Education, Inc.

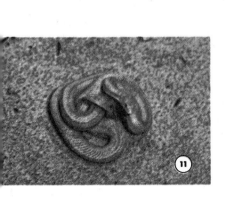

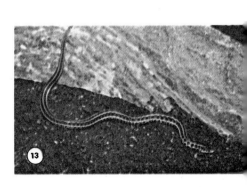

The snapdragon comes from southern Europe

Chicago Natural History Museum
Red snapper

Snapdragon A snapdragon is a flowering garden plant that is grown each year in regions where there is a definite winter. In warm climates or greenhouses, it will live for several years. The slender, rather sticky flowers are in all colors except blue. Snapdragons grow from one to two feet tall.

The asymmetrical flowers grow in clusters on a single stalk. They are perfect, each possessing both male and female structures (stamens and pistil). The pistil matures into a capsule or fruit with many seeds. Each bloom has five petals. The plant gets its name from the fact that the flower snaps open when its sides are pinched.

There are other varieties in addition to the garden variety. Dwarf snapdragons grow to be only six inches tall. Another variety, the *rocket snapdragon*, has long spikes of colorful blossoms.

These HERBS belong to the figwort or Scrophulariaceae family. H. J. C.

Snapper Snappers are deep-bodied, bony fish found in North American tropical waters. Some range as far north as Cape Cod. Most of them are 18 to 36 inches long and weight about two or three pounds.

Snappers are *carnivores* (flesh eaters), feeding upon smaller fish and crustaceans, such as shrimps and crabs. The dorsal fin is more or less continuous; the anterior fin is more coarsely spiny. The anterior part of the anal fin is spiny, but the posterior part is rounded. Of the edible snappers, the *red snapper* from the Gulf of Mexico is most common. J. C. K.

Snapping turtle see Turtle

Sneezewart see Wild flowers

Snipe

Snipe The snipe is one of several long-legged, brownish birds related to the woodcock. It wades in marshes, digging for worms with its long bill.

Snorkel see Submarine

Snow see Precipitation

✳ THINGS TO DO

HOW MUCH SNOW FELL IN YOUR BACKYARD?

1   **Mark inches off on a coffee can starting at the bottom.**
2   **Place the can outside away from the buildings and trees just before a snowstorm has been forecasted.**

3   **You may check your reading by permitting the snow to melt. Ten inches of snow melts down to about one inch of water. Thus there is only one inch of precipitation.**

Snow gauge A snow gauge is an instrument used for measuring snow samples. From the measurement a person can determine the depth of snow and its water equivalent. Such devices were developed around 1910 by a group under the leadership of J. E. Church in Nevada. The need to know how much water was stored in winter snow blankets in the mountains gave rise to the development of the snow gauge. The information was later used to help support life and agriculture in the desert oases and settlements.

Various types of snow gauges exist. In one type the collected snow is melted, poured into the inside tube, and measured by a precisely graduated scale, each graduation being equivalent to 1/100 inch. The depth of snow is the average of measurements taken by some type of ruler or yardstick in a representative exposure. Snow can also be measured by weight. The Universal and Fergusson-type gauges make a continuous record. Rainfall or snow is collected in a receiver that is mounted on a spring balance. The balance positions a pen on a moving chart drum, driven by a clock.

Measuring deep snow, such as in Antarctica, is done by taking a core sample down to rock or by using depth sounding.   D. L. D.

SEE ALSO: WEATHER, WEATHER FORECASTING, WEATHER STATION

Snowberry, or waxberry bush

Snowberry This SHRUB is a hardy, upright plant which grows to be two or more feet tall. It is called *waxberry* in some parts of the United States. LEAVES are simple and one to two inches long. They are arranged in pairs opposite one another on the woody branches. Pink flowers appear in early summer.

Snowberry is a DECIDUOUS bush; it drops its leaves each fall. The leaves have a smooth margin. Each flower is perfect, having both stamens and pistil, and it has five petals that are fused together. The pistil develops into a fleshy fruit that is a white berry. These berries often hang on the branches through the winter months.

Creeping snowberry has slender stems and small evergreen leaves. It forms a mat on the ground and thrives in moist, cool bogs. The flowers are small, white, and bell-shaped. The berries are white and have the fragrance of wintergreen.

Snowberry belongs in the honeysuckle or Caprifoliaceae family.   H. J. C.
SEE ALSO: HONEYSUCKLE, SHRUB

Snowdrop The snowdrop is a small white flower which blooms early in the spring. It looks like a tiny, white bell. Snowdrops may be seen in many parts of the world. They are hardy plants

Snowdrops
Helen J. Challand

which often can be seen blooming through the melting snow.

Snowdrops belong to the *Amaryllis* flower family. The scientific name of snowdrop is *Galanthus*. From its tiny, solid bulb grow two or three long, narrow leaves with parallel veins and rounded tips and a single flower stalk or stem. These plants are easy to grow and grow best in a moist, sunny location.

D. J. A.

Snowline see Mountains

Soap A soap is a cleansing chemical made by cooking an alkali in water solution with fats or oils.

Water alone does not loosen or remove oily or greasy coatings. Soap—discovered by man during the Middle Ages—was found to mix with both water and fatty dirt. It divides the fats into droplets (the *emulsifying action*) and breaks up dark carbon compounds into fine pieces (the *dispersing action*). Chemically, one common soap made from beef fat is *sodium stearate*. The sodium-ion end of the molecule attracts water, and the stearate end attracts soil fats. Warm or hot water plus rubbing and scrubbing help the cleansing action of soap.   D. A. B.
SEE ALSO: DETERGENT, EMULSION, SURFACE TENSION, WETTING AGENT

Soda see Sodium bicarbonate

Sodium (SOH-deeum) Sodium is the most common element of the group known as alkali metals. Sodium metal is very reactive and is never found in its pure state in nature. Sir Humphry Davy, an English chemist, was the first to prepare pure sodium in 1807. Salts of sodium are so common that an unbelievable variety of things in nature contain them.

Pure sodium metal is a soft, silvery substance which reacts violently with water and even with the oxygen in the air. As with other alkali metals, sodium is better known and used more widely in the form of its salts. The following list gives the more familiar of these salts with their uses: *sodium chloride* is common table salt, useful in the human diet and in melting ice and snow on winter streets. *Sodium hy-*

droxide is a caustic or alkaline material used to make soaps and lye, which clean sink drains. *Sodium nitrate* is a fertilizer. *Sodium tetraborate* (borax) is a water softener and cleaner. *Sodium thiosulfate* is used in photography.

Sodium (symbol Na from Latin *natrium*) is element number 11 and has an atomic weight of 22.9898 (22.991, O = 16). Sodium is revealed by a bright yellow flame when its compounds are burned in air.　　M. S.

SEE ALSO: ATOM, ELEMENTS

Sodium bicarbonate (by-KAR-bone-ate) Sodium bicarbonate is one of the most common and most widely used salts of sodium. It is known and sold usually under the name of *baking soda* and is used in baking and as a medicine for stomach upset. It is also called *saleratus*.

Its action in baking depends upon the release of carbon dioxide as a gas. When an acid material such as sour milk is added in the baking process, carbon dioxide is released and trapped in the dough and in this manner causes bread and cakes to rise.

Another name for this material is sodium hydrogen carbonate, and its chemical formula is $NaHCO_3$, molecular weight 84.
　　M. S.

Sodium pentothal Sodium pentothal is a widely used intravenous anesthetic. Because it can produce a hypnotic effect, it is sometimes called "truth serum."

Soft coal see Coal

Soft water see Water

Softwood Trees are divided into two groups: HARDWOOD and softwood. Softwood is wood that can be cut, carved, and worked easily. It is considered to be nonporous. Much of the wood is made of long, empty cells. Softwood trees are generally CONIFERS. Conifers are usually evergreen, such as firs, cedars, pines, and spruces. These trees grow in great forests. They are valuable to mankind as providers of

WHITE FIR

WHITE PINE

REDWOOD

WESTERN HEMLOCK

WESTERN RED CEDAR

LONGLEAF PINE

American Forest Products Industries, Inc.

shelter, fuel, and cool shade. They are useful in the control of floods and soil erosion. They are a very important timber crop. There are over five hundred species of softwood trees and shrubs. They have worldwide distribution.

The long, strong fibers of such softwood trees as the yellow pine, spruce, and fir make them valuable in the manufacture of paper pulp.

Fir trees are good for structural purposes because of their strength and durability. These trees grow to be very large and occur in great quantities. Fir trees can be cut and shipped at reasonable prices. The wood is light and strong. *Douglas fir* is the most commonly used of the fir trees. The wood of the

Douglas fir is used in such structures as ladders, where strength and lightness are necessary. The fir tree is a fine evergreen tree generally found in the temperate zone.

The most widely used woods for telegraph, electric, and telephone poles are the yellow pine, western red and northern cedars, the lodgepole pine, and the Douglas fir. The same trees are used for support or foundation piles. Douglas fir is used in the production of softwood veneers and in the manufacture of interior and exterior PLYWOOD. Fir is sometimes used for making barrels, staves, hogsheads, tanks, vats, shingles, and as a fuel. Its sawdust is used for cleaning and packing.

Cedar trees are handsome evergreen trees. Cedar is the best wood for the manufacture of lead pencils and shingles. It is also used in building, telephone poles, cabinet woods, and cigar boxes. Cedarwood oil is used for pencils, slats, closet linings, and the well-known cedar chests.

Pines are magnificent evergreen trees, valuable as timber and as ornamentals. They are among the most important softwoods used in the manufacture of paper pulp, telephone poles, fiberboards, and insulation. Pine needles are used as a mulch and as a litter for chicken houses. Pines are also used in the manufacture of veneers, shingles, matches, fruit baskets, and wood flour. Wood flour is a finely ground wood used in the manufacture of linoleum and plastics.

Spruce wood is a valuable softwood used in matches, poles, berry baskets, barrel staves, mine timbers, and wood flour. Conifer-leaf oil is extracted from spruce trees and is used in greases, shoe blacking, liniments, and medicines.

Softwoods make up the largest order of GYMNOSPERMS. Gymnosperms appeared abundantly during the Carboniferous Age in the Paleozoic Era of the earth's history. Besides cedar, the most common stands of softwoods today include fir, pine, and spruce, JUNIPER, HEMLOCK, YEW, REDWOOD, and CYPRESS. To date, it appears that the oldest living organism in the world is a softwood: the *Bristle-cone pine* in the White Mountains of California. Scientists have counted as many as forty-six hundred annual rings on one tree. They are older than the sequoia trees (once thought to be the oldest), although they are not as large.   H. J. C.

SEE ALSO: ECONOMIC BOTANY

U.S. Department of Agriculture photo

Soil analysis in the laboratory

Soil testing Soil is tested to find out what kind of chemicals are in the soil. For example, if corn is grown year after year in the same field, certain materials are used up. Farmers need to know what minerals to add. By testing the soil before planting, the farmer can find out what fertilizer to add to replace the minerals that have been used up.

Samples of the soil are taken; and an analysis, or breakdown, of the chemical substances present is made. Conservation departments and farm bureau agents provide this service to individuals requesting it. In some states soil testing has become routine for farmlands, because it is known that different crops remove different kinds and amounts of minerals. Planting certain crops replaces some minerals in the soil.

The major food materials needed by plants are nitrogen, potash, and phosphate. The amount and ratio needed is dependent upon the type of crop and the stage of the growing season. Other substances are required, but in much smaller amounts. These are called *trace* elements. They are also vital to plant growth.

The acidity or basicity (alkalinity) of the soil is determined by testing the *pH* of the soil. On the pH scale, 7 indicates a neutral material. Anything with a pH below 7 is an acid; anything with a pH above 7, a base. Different crops require different soil conditions. Once the pH is known, the soil can be altered for a particular crop. Lawns, for example, often require additional lime to make soil basic. Blueberries, however, require an acid soil, and a basic soil would have to be "soured" for blueberries to do well.   D. J. I.

SEE ALSO: AGRICULTURE, LEGUMES, NITROGEN CYCLE, SOIL TYPES

U.S. Department of Agriculture photo

Good soil for crops has a thick layer of loam, often over sandy soil

Soil types Soil is the name given to worn rock particles of different sizes when they are mixed with decaying or decayed vegetable or animal matter. Generally, the layers of materials found above the solid rocks of the earth are soil. TOPSOIL is the top few inches or feet of soil occupied by plant roots and other living things.

Soil from eroded rocks is distributed about the earth by various geologic agents. Names are used to indicate how soil has been moved. Soil transported by water is referred to as *alluvium*. The term *alluvial plain* refers to a level soil accumulation developed from deposits of soil by overflowing rivers. Airborne soil is called *loess*. Soil which is carried or deposited by glaciers is called *till*.

Soil scientists have listed three primary *soil orders*. The most important of the three is the *zonal order*. It is made up of soils developed over large geographic areas that have had good drainage conditions for long periods of time. The soil-producing processes have made soils with definite horizons. The second is termed the *intrazonal order*. It is made up of soils that are developed under adverse environmental conditions, such as poor drainage. This type of soil is found in swamps and bogs. The third soil order is called *azonal*. It is composed of soils that lack distinct characteristics. Time is required for soils to mature into true soil. Azonal soils

✳ **THINGS TO DO**

DO SOILS VARY IN THE DEGREE TO WHICH THEY HOLD WATER?

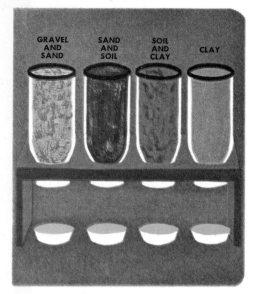

1   **Remove the bottoms from four bottles. Wrap an exposed piece of bell wire around a bottle. Connect the ends of the wire to a series of dry cells. When the wire becomes hot slip the bottle out of the wire ring and immediately immerse it into ice water. The bottom of the bottle will break off. Tape the raw glass.**

2   **Build a small plywood stand to hold the bottles. Tape a piece of gauze over the mouth of each bottle.**

3   **Fill one with gravel and sand, a second one with sand and soil, the third with soil and clay, the fourth with clay. Place dishes under each to catch the drippings.**

4   **With a partner simultaneously pour a cup of water into the top of each bottle. Observe the length of time it takes water to pass through each type of soil.**

5   **Do you think this information is helpful to the farmer?**

have not matured. Since climatic conditions are of major importance in the production of different soil types, soils can generally be classified according to these conditions.

D. J. I.

SEE ALSO: EROSION, GEOLOGY

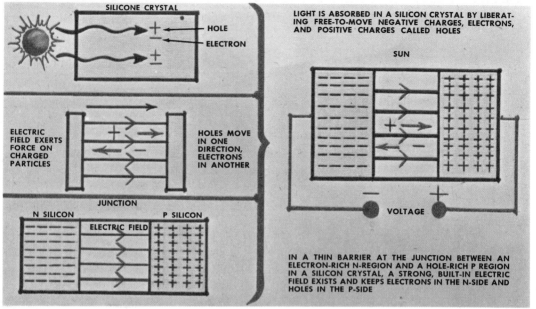

When light is absorbed, freeing electrons and holes in the barrier region at a p-n junction, the built-in electric fields forces the holes into the p-side, making it positive and the electrons into the n-side, making it negative. Displacement of newly-freed charges causes a voltage between the ends of the crystal. Thus light energy is changed to electrical energy

Solar cell A solar cell is a type of electric battery that uses the energy of sunlight to generate electricity. Solar cells can be used in many ways. Now, the solar cell can be used to operate a radio transmitter in an artificial satellite. It is predicted that solar cells will become a major source of energy, replacing coal, oil, and waterpower.

Nearly all energy comes directly or indirectly from the SUN. The energy reaching the earth is radiant energy. If man could store all the radiant energy reaching the earth in three minutes of time, he would have enough to run all his machines and other energy-consuming devices for one year. No one has developed a way to store all of this radiant energy.

The energy running the machines comes from the sun in many other ways. The most common sources of this indirect solar energy are wind, fuels, and water power.

The solar cell is the first attempt by scientists to obtain energy directly from the sun. A small, but practical, solar cell which produces electricity, has been developed by the Bell Telephone Laboratories. The solar cell has been made of specially treated *silicon* crystals.

These slabs of silicon crystal are similar to TRANSISTORS. The crystal has p-type and n-type semiconductor junctions near the surface. Sunlight falling on the silicon crystal surface displaces the electrons from the atoms. Since the junction tends to transport electrons across it in one direction only, an electric current will then flow. Under ideal conditions, nine square feet of silicon crystal in a solar cell will produce 100 watts of electric power. The present solar cells use only about 10% of the solar energy striking their surface.

The first *Vanguard* satellite in 1958 was equipped with solar cells to operate the radio transmitter. Many satellites launched since *Vanguard I* have used solar cells to energize their delicate electronic equipment. Portable radios have been manufactured which utilize solar cells. One telephone system operates on electricity from solar cells. During daylight hours, the solar cells charge storage batteries which then supply current for night telephone operation.   P. F. D.

SEE ALSO: PHOTOELECTRICITY

Solar eclipse see Eclipse

Solar energy see Energy, Solar cell, Sun

Solar plexus The solar plexus is the largest complex of nerves of the sympathetic system. It is located behind the stomach and in front of the aorta.

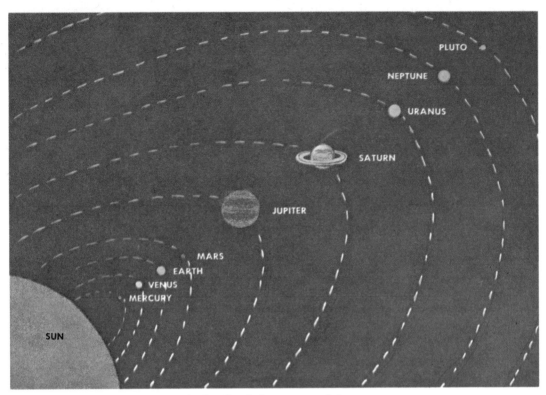

The family of planets around the sun

Solar system The solar system is made up of the sun and its family of heavenly bodies. The sun is the central and largest member of the solar system. The other members revolve around the sun. These other members are the nine known planets, the SATELLITES (*moons*) of some planets, the *asteroids,* and the *comets.*

The word *solar* means *of the sun.* A system, in astronomy, is a group of heavenly bodies that are held together in an organized manner. Solar, the family name of the system to which the Earth belongs, is named for the sun because the sun holds the family together. Most of each member's heat comes from the sun. Wherever the sun moves in space, the rest of the family goes too.

The nine known planets that revolve around the sun are MERCURY, VENUS, EARTH, MARS, JUPITER, SATURN, URANUS, NEPTUNE, and PLUTO. Some of the planets have satellites, which are bodies that revolve around the planets. Each planet controls the orbits of its own satellites by its own mass, though the sun's great pull changes these orbits slightly.

The natural tendency of a planet, because of the combination of motion and mass, would be to travel in a straight line. The gravity of the sun works to pull the planet toward the sun. The gravity of the sun keeps the planet from leaving the solar system. Centrifugal force keeps the planets from being pulled into the sun. The interaction of these two forces keeps the planets in their orbits. They have probably followed the same paths for millions of years and will continue to follow them for many more.

The nine planets that revolve around the sun can be grouped into two classes. The four inner planets (Mercury, Venus, Earth, and Mars) and the outermost planet (Pluto) are called *terrestrial* or earthlike planets. The other planets (Jupiter, Saturn, Uranus, and

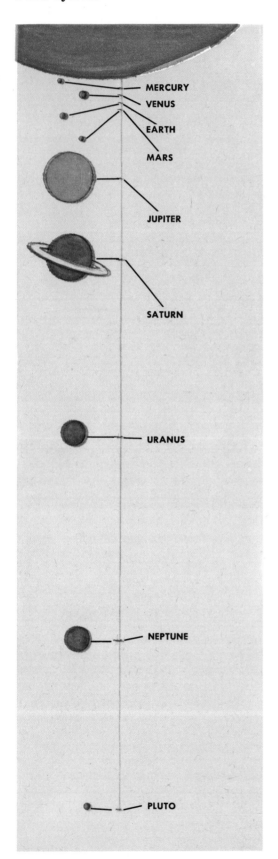

MERCURY
VENUS
EARTH
MARS

JUPITER

SATURN

URANUS

NEPTUNE

PLUTO

Neptune) are in the other class, the *gas giants*. The terrestrial planets are relatively small and solid. The gas giants are truly gigantic compared with the smaller planets. They may have solid cores, but they are surrounded by very deep atmospheres of gases mostly unlike man's air.

All of the planets move around the sun in the same direction—from east to west. There are some short periods of exception to this rule. When Uranus, for example, is near Neptune, Uranus is influenced by Neptune's gravity. Uranus slows down and appears to move backward for awhile. This is called a *perturbation* of Uranus' orbit.

The orbits of the planets are not perfectly circular. They are elliptical. The inner planets follow more nearly circular paths than the outer planets. Pluto's path is very elongated and eccentric. Most of the planets travel along orbits that are nearly in the same plane or level. Pluto, again, is least like the others. Its orbit is tilted more than any other planet's. The shape of the solar system itself is somewhat like a saucer. Its width is about 6,000 million miles.

The planets move at different speeds. Mercury, the planet closest to the sun, makes the shortest trip and travels fastest. Pluto takes the longest time to complete a journey around the sun. The distance from the sun greatly influences the speed at which a planet moves.

There is a fairly regular scheme of gaps between the orbits of the planets. Johann Bode, a German astronomer, figured out this system and noticed that there was a planet missing from his scheme between Mars and Jupiter. In the area where, according to Bode's law, there should have been a planet, thousands of tiny bodies have been discovered. These asteroids or *minor planets* orbit around the sun. They are large rocks and smaller pebble-like particles—METEORS. The ASTEROIDS might once have been a planet that burst apart or they might be pieces of material that never came together to form a planet. Occasionally a meteor strays into the atmosphere of Earth and glows like a "falling star."

Besides the planets and asteroids, there are other members of the sun's family. These are the COMETS. They travel in very long elliptical orbits and are not always in the same plane as the planets. Comets have a

✳ **THINGS TO DO**

BUILDING PLANETS FROM MERCURY TO PLUTO

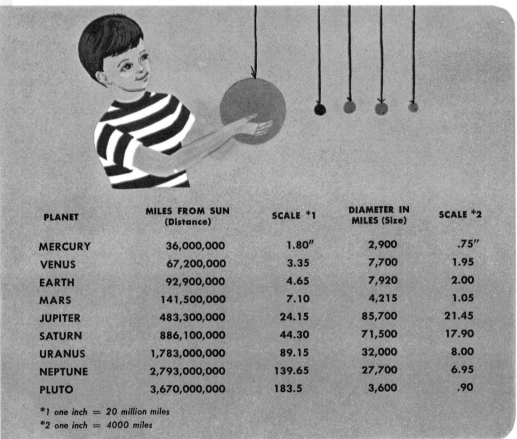

PLANET	MILES FROM SUN (Distance)	SCALE *1	DIAMETER IN MILES (Size)	SCALE *2
MERCURY	36,000,000	1.80″	2,900	.75″
VENUS	67,200,000	3.35	7,700	1.95
EARTH	92,900,000	4.65	7,920	2.00
MARS	141,500,000	7.10	4,215	1.05
JUPITER	483,300,000	24.15	85,700	21.45
SATURN	886,100,000	44.30	71,500	17.90
URANUS	1,783,000,000	89.15	32,000	8.00
NEPTUNE	2,793,000,000	139.65	27,700	6.95
PLUTO	3,670,000,000	183.5	3,600	.90

*1 one inch = 20 million miles
*2 one inch = 4000 miles

1 In order to see the relationship in the size of planets and their relative distance from the sun you can construct models to scale.

2 The accompanying chart provides the diameter of the planets and the number of inches each model should be made when one inch equals approximately 4000 miles.

3 Models made of papier maché (newspaper strips and paste) can be used.

For large planets, blow up balloons to one inch less than desired size. Mold a half-inch of papier maché over the balloon and let it dry.

4 The planets may be suspended by strings from the ceiling of the room. Arrange them in order from the sun by following the chart. The scale for distance is based upon one inch equaling 20 million miles. Moons and other bodies may be added.

bright head and a long shining tail. They shine partly by light absorbed from the sun and then reradiated and partly by reflected sunlight.

None of the other bodies that revolve around the sun reradiate sunlight. They all shine by reflecting light from the sun.

Quite a few members of the solar system can be observed without the aid of a telescope. With the naked eye, one can see the sun and the moon, occasionally a meteor or "falling star," once in a great while a comet, and five of the planets. These five planets are Mercury, Venus, Mars, Jupiter, and Saturn. These planets cannot all be seen on the same night. Two of them spotted in one night is a good score. With the naked eye, they look very much like stars. With a telescope, however, they show up as disks of light, while the biggest stars appear only as points of

Ancient people first named certain heavenly bodies "planets"

light. As the planets move along their journeys around the sun, their positions in our sky change. They move from constellation to constellation. Ancient people noticed these "wandering stars" and named them "planets," which means "wanderers." If a person wants to observe a planet, with only his eyes or with a telescope, he needs to know where and when to look for it.

One will never see a planet in the northern sky—around Ursa Major (the BIG DIPPER), for instance. Since most of the members of the solar system move in about the same plane, the planets follow the same path across the sky that the sun traces out. A narrow band of constellations that forms a background for the apparent paths of the sun, the moon, and the planets, is called the ZODIAC.

Many years ago men believed that the earth was the center of the universe. They thought that the sun, the MOON, the stars, and the visible planets revolved around the earth. COPERNICUS introduced the idea that the sun was the center of the system. When the telescope was invented, GALILEO used facts that he had discovered with the telescope to support the new theory. Tycho Brahe and JOHANNES KEPLER went on to make the picture of the solar system more accurate. Kepler's calculations from Brahe's data showed that the planets do not travel in perfect circles around the sun. SIR ISAAC NEWTON determined the laws of gravity which help to explain how the system is held together. Later astronomers kept on working to make knowledge about the solar system more accurate. They studied the sizes, motions, compositions, and conditions of the other planets. They discovered planets in the system that early astronomers did not know

about. Man-made satellites and planetary probes will add more to the knowledge about the solar system. Men are studying how to leave Earth and explore the system.

The SUN is a star—a typical, average star. It is not remarkable for its size, or age, or brightness. Astronomers and nonastronomers alike have wondered whether the sun is an unusual star · because it has a system of bodies that revolve around it. There are undoubtedly many other stars in the universe that have systems similar to the one in which man travels.

If astronomers could determine how the solar system was formed, they would be better able to estimate how many other stars have planetary systems. Several theories have been suggested about how the solar system was born. One theory is that the sun and the planets, millions of years ago, were an enormous gas cloud or nebula. The cloud was whirling very rapidly. Some of the matter condensed to form the sun. Some was thrown off in rings that spun around the sun. The material in the rings condensed to form the planets which continued to follow the paths of the rings. Another theory is that the planets were formed when the sun and another star collided in space, or had perhaps merely a near-collision. This theory supposes that another star got so near the sun that its gravity pulled matter away from the sun and this matter formed the planets. Still another theory is similar to the ring-theory. It says that after the sun was formed it had a flattened gas cloud circling around it. The cloud became separated in great whirlpools of gases and solid matter which whirled around the sun. As the whirlpools spun around, dust and lumps of matter hit each other and became packed into the individual planets. None of these theories has been proved.

When astronomers try to explain the birth of the solar system, they have to take into account several facts. The first is that the planets and the sun are nearly in the same plane. The second is the fact that the planets and satellites have predominantly east to west rotational and revolutional motions. Last, the orbits have similar shapes and are regularly distributed as Bode described.   C. L. K.

SEE ALSO: ASTRONOMY, CONSTELLATIONS, GRAVITY, MILKY WAY, MOON, PLANETS, SATELLITE, SPACE

Solar system, origin of Since 1790 scholars have tried to explain the origin of the solar system. Among these was Pierre Simon de Laplace who said the solar system began with a large cloud of gas. His idea was called the *nebular theory.*

In 1900, Chamberlin and Moulton suggested that another large star had crashed into the sun and had torn off bits of gases which became planets. This was called the *planetesimal* theory.

About the same time Jeans and Jefferies taught that another large sun approaching the sun now circled by Earth, caused a large wave, and when the wave broke up the planets were formed. This was called the *tidal* theory.

Much has been learned since that time by astronomers. It is now known that none of these theories is a satisfactory explanation of the origin of the solar system. Since 1944 astronomers are inclined to return to the nebula or gas-cloud theory with many changes in the light of new discoveries.

Present-day astronomers who have proposed hypotheses relating to the contraction of a large nebula to form the sun and a gaseous disk from which the planets evolved include von Weizsacker, Kuiper, and Hoyle.

The nebular idea (hypothesis) of Laplace suggested that the solar system was once a large cloud of hot gaseous material. As this gaseous material rotated and contracted, a large disk formed around a central point. The central point became a new star, the sun. The disk around the sun contracted, causing the formation of rings and gases from time to time which were detached from the main disk. These separate rings formed the planets as they contracted. Laplace believed that the rings of SATURN were proof.

The planetesimal hypothesis suggests that a close encounter (or actual collision) took place between the sun and another star. This encounter tore off fragments of the sun. Some fragments cooled and condensed, forming the cores of the planets. The cores attracted additional material and grew.

The tidal theory of Jeans and Jefferies states that the approach of another sun set up a huge tidal wave on the sun's surface. As the tidal wave broke up, the planets were formed eventually.

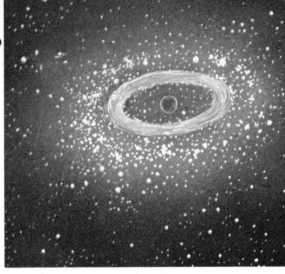

Formation of the solar system according to the LaPlace theory

The nebular hypothesis of LAPLACE explained quite well the high speed of rotation of the planets and that all the planets except URANUS rotate and revolve in the same direction. It does not, however, account for the very slow period of rotation of the sun. The sun rotates in 26 days, but it should rotate in about one-half day according to the principle of conservation of angular momentum.

The *nebular contraction* hypothesis of von Weizsacker states that the particles of gaseous material in the disk around the sun would move in orbits shaped like kidney beans. This orbit of the particles would be with respect to each other, yet the orbit of each particle with respect to the sun itself would be elliptical. Weizsacker further assumes the five kidney bean-shaped orbits formed around the sun in a string and successive strings of five formed at other distances from the sun. Between the successive strings collisions of particles occurred and the particles stuck together. As this mass of material grew, its gravitational attraction hastened the formation of larger masses.

Kuiper bases his hypothesis on a disk around a newly-formed sun. He also suggests kidney bean eddies, but believes the eddies would be more irregular. Kuiper's hypothesis does not agree that the planets evolved from a gradual accumulation, but rather that the planets evolved from two opposing forces acting on the eddies of gas in the disk. These forces are the gravitation of the sun and the gravity of the disk itself. When great enough, the gravity of the disk formed a *protoplanet.*   J. H. D.

SEE ALSO: EARTH, EARLY DEVELOPMENT OF; STARS; SUN

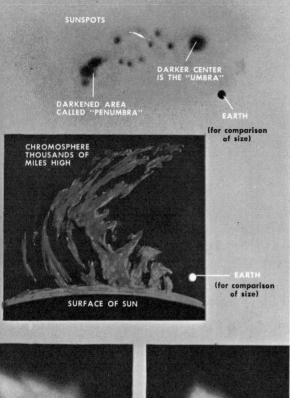

SUNSPOTS

DARKER CENTER IS THE "UMBRA"

DARKENED AREA CALLED "PENUMBRA"

EARTH
(for comparison of size)

CHROMOSPHERE THOUSANDS OF MILES HIGH

EARTH
(for comparison of size)

SURFACE OF SUN

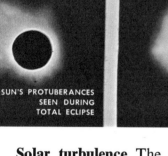

SUN'S PROTUBERANCES SEEN DURING TOTAL ECLIPSE

Solar turbulence The surface of the sun shows much activity and change, or *turbulence.* On the *photosphere,* the bright surface layer that is seen, *sunspots, flares* and *gas streams* occur. By observing sunspots and other activity, astronomers have been able to tell that the sun rotates and that it is not a solid body.

Sunspots appear as darkened areas with darker centers. The spots have a temperature 2000° K less than the surrounding surface, which has a temperature of about 6000° K. As swirling magnetic storms, they usually travel in pairs across the sun.

The *chromosphere,* a layer of gases which appears reddish in color due to its composition of hydrogen and helium, extends for several thousand miles above the photosphere. Prominences of the chromosphere can be viewed during an eclipse, when the sun's main disk is blocked off entirely by the moon. They also may be viewed by a telescopic attachment called a *coronagraph.* This device keeps just a thin rim of the chromosphere in view, and permits only red hydrogen light to pass into a camera to be recorded.

Photographs of the chromosphere show streamers of glowing gas and other clouds erupting with great speed to fly away from the surface. At times, these travel out half a million miles.

In the area of sunspots there are loop-shaped fountains of gas. Some twisted columns appear like tornados and soon disappear; others take the shape of haystacks and have the longest life.

The smallest features of the photosphere are the giant grainy masses which cover over one-third of the surface. A series of enlarged photos show these to be constantly changing. Their size is about 700 miles across each grain.

The sun's *corona* is actually a thin atmosphere extending out into the solar system. It gives feeble light near the body of the sun. The outer parts are streamers that range out to a million miles.   F. R. W.

SEE ALSO: SUN

Soldering (SOD-er-ing) Soldering is a process in which a metal with a low melting point is used to join two other metals. The solder is heated, the parts to be joined are warmed, and the solder hardens in place when applied.

SEE: ALLOY

Sole (SOHL) Sole refers to any of several kinds of excellent food flatfish found in temperate and tropical waters. Sole was originally the name of the common European sole, but the classification has been extended to include any of the edible flatfish like the FLOUNDER.

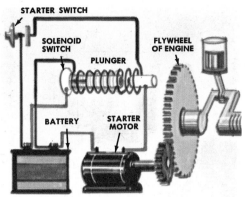

THE SOLENOID MAKES CONTACT FOR HEAVY CURRENT TO TURN THE STARTER MOTOR WHEN A REMOTE CONTROL SWITCH MOVES PLUNGER

Solenoid (SOH-luh-noid) A solenoid is a tubular coil of wire which produces a magnetic field when current is passed through the wire. The magnetic field is strongest inside the coil and at the ends; the field is weakest outside the coil.

One of the simplest forms is the plunger-type solenoid. A soft-iron rod or plunger is held just outside one end of the cylinder. When the electrical current passes through the coil, the magnetic field pulls the plunger into the coil.

The solenoid is an important part of many electrical devices. Many types of circuit breakers, relays, and contactors use solenoids. In these devices, electrical contacts open or close depending on the presence or absence of a control current in the solenoid coil.

When electrical current used in a signal system has to be changed from one voltage to another, solenoids are employed in a transformer relay system. Some fire alarm systems found in public buildings use this type of solenoid. Old fire alarm systems have low-voltage equipment. Rather than rewire the entire system when a new addition is added to a building, the lower voltage alarm system is connected to the newer 110-voltage alarm system by solenoid relays.

Many conveyor belt systems employ solenoids for sorting out imperfect items. Automobiles, electric eye systems, and telephone relays use solenoids.   P. F. D.

SEE ALSO: AUTOMATION; ELECTROMAGNET; SWITCHES, ELECTRIC; TRANSFORMER

Solid A solid in GEOMETRY is a part of space with three dimensions— length, breadth, and thickness. In physics, a solid is a state of matter in which a substance possesses definite and distinct volume and shape.

SEE: PHYSICAL STATES AND CHANGES

Solo man see Evolution of man

Solstice (SAHL-stihs) The solstices are the two times of the year when the sun appears highest and lowest in the sky. These are also times of the longest and shortest days. Solstices occur three months from the equinoxes, when days are of equal length.

There are two solstices. The summer solstice, which occurs about June 21, is celebrated in parts of Europe as midsummer's day. This celebration stems from primitive, religious rites of early sun worshippers. On this day the sun appears in the sky for a longer time than on any other day. From June 21 until about December 22, the winter solstice, the length of the days shortens. Thus the December solstice also had significance for early people because it marked the beginning of winter.

The sun's apparent position shifts in the Earth's sky because Earth is tilted at an angle of 23½ degrees on its axis. As Earth proceeds in its path about the sun, the distance of the sun to certain geographical areas and the angle of the sun's rays entering the atmosphere vary. Thus, in winter, the Northern Hemisphere points away from the sun. The sun then appears low in the sky, even at noon. In summer, the northern part is on the side tilting toward the sun. Then the sun appears higher in the sky, and, at noon, almost overhead.   D. J. I.

SEE ALSO: ASTRONOMY, EQUINOX, SEASONS

Courtesy Society For Visual Education, Inc.

24 hours of daylight in N. polar regions

Summer long days short nights

warmest direct rays from sun

Winter short days long nights

24 hours of night in S. polar regions

June Solstice

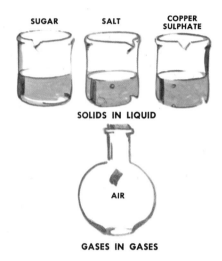

SUGAR SALT COPPER SULPHATE

SOLIDS IN LIQUID

AIR

GASES IN GASES

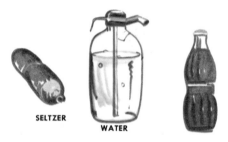

ALCOHOL + WATER
LIQUID IN LIQUID

SELTZER WATER

GAS IN LIQUID

BRASS IS A SOLUTION OF COPPER AND ZINC

SOLID IN SOLID (after hardening)

A variety of types of solutions can be made using different physical states of matter as the solvent and solute. There are limitations: a solid cannot be dissolved in a gas; some materials can be dissolved only at certain temperatures

Solubility (sol-yuh-BIL-i-ty) Solubility is the amount of a substance (SOLUTE) which will dissolve in a given amount of another substance (SOLVENT). It is expressed usually as the number of parts of solute by weight dissolved by 100 parts of solvent.

Solute (SOL-oot) A solute is a substance which is able to dissolve in another, usually larger amount of a substance. Gases and solids are usually the solutes when combined with liquids. They are dispersed or scattered in the SOLVENT.
SEE: DISPERSION

Solution (suh-LOO-shun) When the atoms or molecules of one substance are spread uniformly throughout those of another substance, the result is a *solution.* One substance is then *dissolved* in the other. The substance present in smaller amount is the SOLUTE. The substance present in larger amount is the SOLVENT. In a sugar-water solution, the sugar is the solute, the water is the solvent.

Sand and sugar can be mixed, shaken, and stirred, but one does not dissolve in the other. This MIXTURE is *heterogeneous,* which means that the two parts of the mixture are different from each other. Sand and sugar cannot be made to go into solution. If sand is put into a container of water, the sand still does not dissolve. If the container is shaken, the sand may spread through the water. The mixture feels gritty, but it is easy enough to separate the sand from the water. If the mixture is allowed to stand for a while, the sand will settle out. Sand and water do not make a solution. If sugar is put into water, however, the sugar does dissolve. The sugar becomes so well mixed with the water that the individual grains of sugar can no longer be seen. The mixture is *homogeneous.* It is a solution.

Liquid solutions can be made using a solid, liquid, or gas as the solute. Alcohol and water, for example, dissolve in each

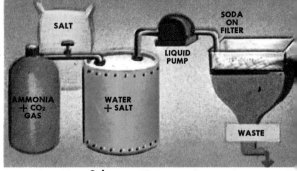
Solvay process

other. Solid solutions also can be made using a solid, liquid, or gas as the solute. Brass is a solution (ALLOY) of two solids—copper and zinc.

Stirring or shaking make a solute dissolve faster. Also, the greater the solute surface exposed to the solvent, the faster the solution is formed. A lump or a large crystal of sugar dissolves more slowly than does the same weight of fine-grained sugar.

A solute dissolves in a heated solvent faster. This result is predicted by the KINETIC-MOLECULAR THEORY. Heating also makes most solids dissolve in greater amount than the same solids do in colder solvent. A few solids, calcium hydroxide, for instance, dissolve best in cold water. Gases dissolve in greater concentration in cold solvents. Boiling a solution of a gas and water causes the gas to leave the solution first. Pressure increases the solubility of gases in liquids. In carbonated drinks, carbon dioxide is kept in solution under pressure. When the cap is removed from the bottle, the pressure is released and bubbles of carbon dioxide escape.

There is a limit to the amount of solute a given quantity of solvent can contain at a given temperature. If a very small amount of salt is dissolved in a large container of water, the solution is called a *dilute* solution. If a greater quantity of salt is added and dissolved, the solution is *concentrated*. When the limit is reached and the water has dissolved all the salt it can take, the solution reaches a point of *saturation*. Heating the salt water allows more salt to dissolve. If this hot solution is then allowed to crystallize slowly, the excess salt may not settle. This solution is *super-saturated* because it contains more solute than ordinarily can be dissolved in that amount of solvent at that temperature.   C. L. K.

Solvay process (SOL-vay) The Solvay process is a chemical process used in the manufacture of sodium carbonate (commonly known as *washing soda* or *sal soda*) and SODIUM BICARBONATE (a household product familiar as baking soda). This process was perfected in 1863 by two Belgians, Ernest and Alfred Solvay. It uses cheap and abundant materials.

In this process carbon dioxide and ammonia gases are passed upward under pressure through a concentrated solution of salt (sodium chloride). Carbon dioxide, ammonia and water form ammonium carbonate:

$$CO_2 + 2NH_3 + H_2O \rightarrow (NH_4)_2CO_3$$

The latter reacts with the salt to form sodium carbonate and ammonium chloride:

$$(NH_4)_2CO_3 + 2NaCl \rightarrow Na_2CO_3 + 2NH_4Cl.$$

Finally sodium carbonate reacts with carbon dioxide to form sodium bicarbonate:

$$Na_2CO_3 + CO_2 + H_2O \rightarrow 2NaHCO_3$$

The sodium bicarbonate is precipitated out, filtered, and dried. It is then heated to a dull red heat, to form sodium carbonate.

$$2NaHCO_3 + heat \rightarrow Na_2CO_3 + H_2O + CO_2\uparrow$$

This regenerative process is very economical because it reuses most of the by-products.

The ammonium chloride produced is heated with slaked lime [$Ca(OH_2)$] to produce ammonia, which is passed into the reaction chambers and reused.

$$Ca(OH_2) + 2NH_4Cl \rightarrow CaCl_2 + 2H_2O + 2NH_3\uparrow$$

Slaked lime is made by heating limestone ($CaCO_3$) which gives carbon dioxide and lime, and then treated with water.

$$CaCO_3 + heat \rightarrow CaO + CO_2\uparrow$$
$$(lime)$$
$$CaO + H_2O \rightarrow Ca(OH)_2$$

The carbon dioxide released is reused directly in the process. *Chlorine* is produced from the waste calcium chloride by *electrolysis*.
                                        D. L. D.

SEE ALSO: AMMONIA

Solvent (SOL-vunt) A solvent is a kind of liquid substance which is able to dissolve another substance (SOLUTE). Usually the solvent is present in greater amount than the solute. A liquid is often the solvent for a solid, a gas, or another liquid.

SEE: SOLUTION

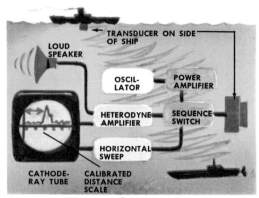

LOUD SPEAKER

TRANSDUCER ON SIDE OF SHIP

OSCIL-LATOR

POWER AMPLIFIER

HETERODYNE AMPLIFIER

SEQUENCE SWITCH

HORIZONTAL SWEEP

CATHODE-RAY TUBE

CALIBRATED DISTANCE SCALE

Diagram of sonar process

Sonar (SOH-nahr) Sonar is an electronic device that detects objects in the ocean through the use of sound. Sonar determines the object's location by sending vibrations. These vibrations are reflected back to the sonar device after they strike the object. Military ships and airplanes use sonar to find the location of enemy submarines. Ships employ sonar to determine the depth of the water beneath their keels. "Sonar" is composed of the first letters of each of the words "Sound," "Navigation," "And," and "Range."

Sonar consists of the *transmitter,* the *transducer,* the receiver, and the indicator. The transmitter sends electrical signals to the transducer. The transducer is an antenna-like apparatus submerged in the water. Electric signals from the transmitter go to the transducer and are converted into sound waves. The sound waves use frequencies between 5,000 and 25,000 cycles per second.

Upon striking a submarine or the ocean bottom, the sound waves return to the ship's sonar device. The sound waves picked up by the receiver are timed by the indicator. Sound travels at the rate of about 5000 feet per second in water. The indicator automatically translates the returning sound waves into a computed distance, thus determining the location of the submarine or the depth to the ocean floor.   P. F. D.

SEE ALSO: DEPTH SOUNDING, RADIO, SOUND

Song sparrow see Finch

Sonic barrier When an aircraft accelerates to and beyond the speed of sound, it is said to cross the "sound barrier." Great stress is placed on the aircraft at the moment it pushes beyond its own shock waves, and a "sonic boom," or explosive-like noise, results when they reach the ground.

Sonic boom see Supersonic

Sore throat A sore throat is a painful inflammation of the tonsils or of the mucous membrane of the *pharynx*—the cavity directly behind the nose and mouth.

Sorghum (SORE-gum) Sorghum is a cereal grass that occurs in many varieties.

There are four main groups. The *sweet* sorghums are used for making molasses or syrup and for feeding cattle and horses. The *grain* sorghums are used for food for man and animals. The *grass* sorghums are used mainly for making hay. The *broomcorn* sorghums are used for making brooms and brushes. Grain sorghums are now being used in several industrial processes as a source of starch, wax, and other products.

The crop is raised like corn. Its tall plants, which grow from eight to 15 feet, have plumy seed heads at the top. Sorghum grows best in areas that have long, hot summers, and in rich garden soil, or in sandy soils, such as in the southeastern United States. The plant needs regular cultivation.

Sorghum is susceptible to rusts, smut, insect pests, and fungous diseases.   M. R. L.

SEE ALSO: CEREAL GRAINS, GRASSES

Sorghum grasses

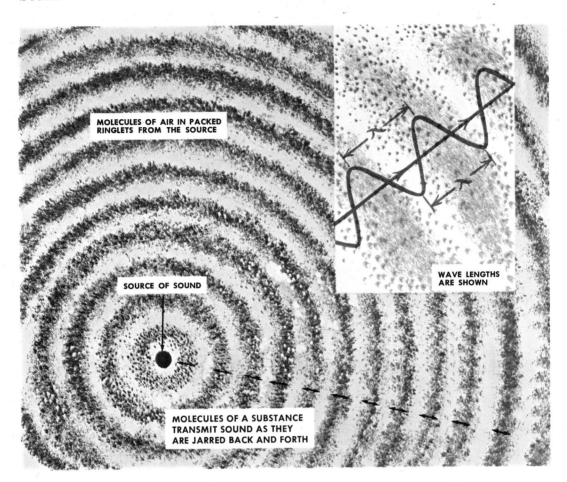

MOLECULES OF AIR IN PACKED RINGLETS FROM THE SOURCE

WAVE LENGTHS ARE SHOWN

SOURCE OF SOUND

MOLECULES OF A SUBSTANCE TRANSMIT SOUND AS THEY ARE JARRED BACK AND FORTH

The arrows shown indicate only the vibration back and forth. Sound from the source is vibrating and traveling in all directions

Sound Sound is a form of energy. When something moves back and forth, it is a *vibration*. Many vibrations moving through a material make waves. When these waves are of the right frequency, they are picked up by the ear and sent to the brain, and sound is heard.

Sounds move in all directions through a material. They will go through many materials such as air, water, metals, wood, and cloth. Sounds can be made by striking, plucking, blowing, scraping, and in other ways. They may be loud, soft, high, low, pleasant, or unpleasant.

Animals make sounds in different ways. Crickets, grasshoppers, and katydids rub together the small projections on their wings, thus setting them in motion. *Cicadas* have a thin membrane over small depres-

sions on the lower abdomen. They are able to vibrate these membranes by muscular contractions. The hum of mosquitoes and flies is produced by the fast movement of their wings.

Among the *vertebrates,* some fish will forcibly expel air from their swim bladders, making a distinct sound. *Amphibians* were the first vocal vertebrates, having a *larynx* and vocal cords. Reptiles lack these, but the snake forces air out in a hissing noise, whereas the alligator bellows. Birds have a special voice organ, the *syrinx,* a membrane located at the lower end of the *trachea.* This is set in motion as air is expelled. Mammals including man have the most complete sound-making mechanism and produce the widest variety of sounds.

Animals receive and interpret sound waves by special structures called EARS. These organs in man enable him to hear sound if the range frequency falls between

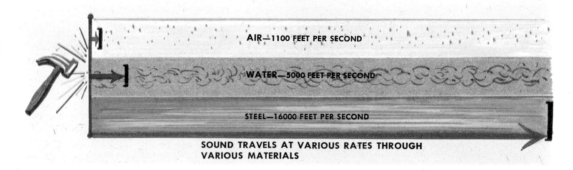

AIR—1100 FEET PER SECOND

WATER—5000 FEET PER SECOND

STEEL—16000 FEET PER SECOND

**SOUND TRAVELS AT VARIOUS RATES THROUGH
VARIOUS MATERIALS**

**The speed of a sound wave is increased considerably in solid materials, as the sound bounces back
and forth between more compressed particles**

20 to 20,000 vibrations per second. The direction of the source of the sound is determined by the slight difference in the time for the sound to reach both ears.

SOUND WAVES

Any material that can vibrate can make waves. When the molecules in a material are pushed together, they, in turn, push on the molecules next to them. The molecules that first were pressed together will move back quickly into the space from which they started, and the molecules that were displaced will push on the next group. This makes the first wave. Each group of molecules pushing on the next group and then bouncing back gives a wave. At each place and at each time this back and forth movement happens, a wave exists.

When waves are longitudinal—that is, when the molecules vibrate along a straight line, parallel to the direction that the wave travels—they are classified as *sound waves.* Sound waves in a given medium (such as air) are progressive movements of varying lengths. The patterns of sound waves is determined by the force applied to the material to be set in motion and by the size, shape, and kind of material used to make a sound.

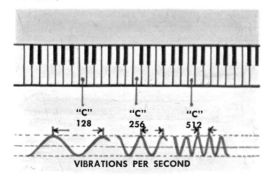

"C" "C" "C"
128 256 512

VIBRATIONS PER SECOND

Waves will travel in all directions from a source of sound, up and down, and around corners. Sound travels through solids, liquids, or gases. It cannot travel through a VACUUM since there are no molecules to move. Sound travels through materials at different rates of speed, depending upon their density and temperature. In still air at 45° F., sound travels 1100 feet per second, or a mile in five seconds. As compared with the speed of LIGHT rays, this is slow. Light travels over 982,000 times faster than sound, which explains why one sees lightning before hearing the thunder. Sound waves move five times faster in water than in air, and 15 times faster in steel than in air. Waves going through warm air travel faster than those going through cold air.

FREQUENCY

Sounds are made in a variety of ways with many kinds of materials. *Frequency* is defined as the number of vibrations per second. Wave lengths are measured in meters, centimeters, or feet. A meter is 39.37 inches. The shorter the wave length, the greater the frequency or pitch.

The loudness of a sound as heard depends on two factors. One is the distance between the object which is causing the vibration and the receiving organ, the ear. The second factor is the force used in making the sound. When a string on a MUSICAL INSTRUMENT is tapped lightly, it will move up and down very little. When struck forcibly, the string will vibrate the same number of times per second (same pitch) but will have greater *amplitude,* thus making the sound louder.

AMPLITUDE

Amplitude in connection with sound re-

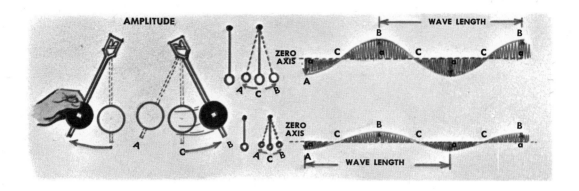

fers to the maximum distance a vibrating particle moves away or is displaced from its position of rest or equilibrium. Consider, for example, a weight on a piece of string such as seen above. This is a condition similar to the pendulum of a clock. The position where the weight comes to rest or equilibrium is at *C*. If the weight is set into motion by pulling it aside and releasing it, the pendulum will swing to and fro or oscillate with an amplitude which is equal to either *CA* or *CB,* since *A* and *B* are the points of swing furthest from *C*.

Because sound is thought of as traveling in waves, the amplitude of the swinging weight must be related to the amplitude of a wave. A comparison of the two is made above. Here it is seen that if the oscillations of the weight were to be plotted against time, they would take the form of a wave as shown. Hence, the amplitude of a wave is the distance from the zero point or zero axis to the peak of the wave. In the figure this is shown as dimension *a*.

As the ear receives a sound, the amplitude depends upon three factors. The first is the amplitude of the vibrating body itself. The second is the area surrounding the vibrating object, and the third is the distance from the object to the point of the observer. All of these conditions which affect the amplitude are also directly responsible for the intensity or loudness of a sound.

AIR COLUMN

The method of producing sound by using a column of air is similar to that used in producing sound with a stringed musical instrument, such as a violin.

Instead of having a string which vibrates and in turn produces sound waves, the air in the column is set into motion directly by a vibrating object, such as a reed. Just as the violinist uses the bow to set the strings of a violin in motion, a blast or jet of air against the reed causes a disturbance of the air in the column and creates the sound.

Since the air in a column or tube is restricted by the walls and ends of the container, it can vibrate only in a certain way. When the blast of air travels across the reed, the resulting disturbance moves down the tube, is bounced from the opposite end, and returns to the reed end. A simple demonstration of this is to take an empty soda pop bottle and blow across the mouth

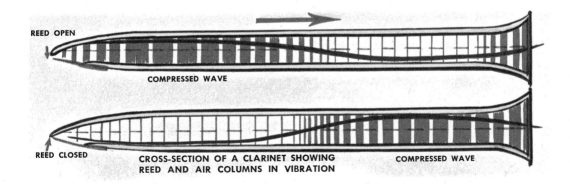

CROSS-SECTION OF A CLARINET SHOWING
REED AND AIR COLUMNS IN VIBRATION

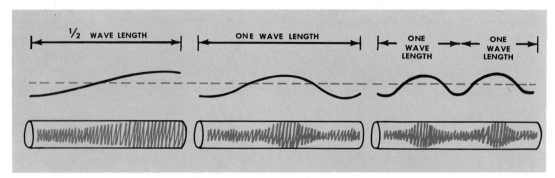

½ WAVE LENGTH　　ONE WAVE LENGTH　　ONE WAVE LENGTH　　ONE WAVE LENGTH

Pitch or frequency range of sound varies the wave length

of the bottle. In this case the lips act as the reed and the bottle as the tube containing the air column.

The principal condition which determines the pitch or frequency (and hence the wave length) of the sound produced by an air column is the length of the tube.

At the closed end of the tube no vibration can take place because this is a rigid or fixed end. Consequently, the closed end of the tube must be a place where no movement occurs. Places where no vibration occurs are called *nodes*.

Similarly, because the mouth of the tube is open it must be the place of greatest or maximum movement, so it is called an *antinode* or loop in a string. Thus the disturbance created in the tube is a wave consisting of nodes and antinodes.

There can be more than one node or antinode present in the tube. A tube resonating in its fundamental frequency may have a node and antinode present. Another tube three times longer than the first tube may have two nodes and two antinodes. Still another tube five times longer than the first tube contains three nodes and three antinodes.

The property of overtones in air columns is extremely useful in producing musical instruments which will give full, rich tones. Organ pipes, clarinets, and brass horns are all good examples of musical instruments employing air columns. Some instruments have tubes which are open at both ends. When this is true, there must be an antinode at each end. Also, for any sound to be produced there must be a nodal point somewhere in the tube. The proper place for this is in the center of the tube when the tube is resonating in its fundamental frequency. In the drawing above, an open pipe

is represented with a wave of the fundamental frequency. It shows a pipe of the same length but containing the first overtone of the fundamental frequency, and likewise the illustration shows the second overtone.

ACOUSTICS

Acoustics deals mainly with the quality of sound received by the ear. Many of the physical laws which govern these particular properties of sound are by no means simple and have been arrived at mainly through experiment.

The term "loudness" has no definite physical value, because this is a psychological experience. It depends upon the mechanical properties of the ear and the sensing elements of the brain. Since no two people hear exactly the same, a particular sound may seem louder to one person than to another. There is no such thing as an "absolute" value for loudness, but the difference between the loudness of two sounds can be measured. The unit of difference of loudness is called a *bel,* after Alexander Graham Bell, the inventor of the telephone. This unit, from the nature of its derivation, is large so that another, more common, unit is often used—1/10 of a bel or a *decibel.*

In connection with loudness, there exists what is called the *threshold of audibility.* For a sound to be heard at all it must exceed a certain minimum intensity. The commonly used threshold value of intensity is 10^{-16} watt/cm² at 20° C. There is also a certain upper limit to the intensity a sound can have and still be called sound in the usual sense of the word. Any sound which has an intensity of over 130 decibels is usually considered a painful sound. The sound is painful because the pressure created by the

FINDING OUT ABOUT SOUND

A WILL SOUND TRAVEL THROUGH LIQUIDS?

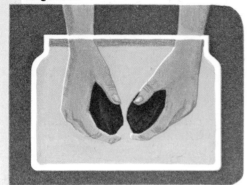

Fill a large pail or other container with water. Hold two rocks down in the water and strike them together forcibly. Did you hear a sound?

B WILL SOUND PASS THROUGH SOLIDS?

Put your ear close to the end of a wooden table. Ask another person to scratch the wood at the opposite end with a fingernail or other sharp object. Can you hear a sound through the wood?

C DOES THE SIZE OF AN OBJECT AFFECT THE PITCH OF SOUND?

Use a teaspoon and a tablespoon for this experiment. Strike each one on the same kind of material. Which one makes a higher sound?

D DO SOUNDS GO IN ALL DIRECTIONS?

Stand outside in a busy place and listen for all kinds of sounds. Are sounds coming up to your ears from the ground? Can you hear any sounds coming out of the sky down to you? What noises are to the sides, the back, and the front of you? Can you hear sounds from objects you can't see such as the fire engine coming down another street. Does this prove that sound travels around corners?

E DOES THE DENSITY OF A MATERIAL AFFECT THE SPEED OF SOUND?

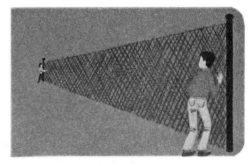

This experiment requires a length of metal at least 75 feet long. An iron fence will have continuous rods running through it or a roll of wire may be stretched the length of your backyard or school ground. Stand at one end with a partner at the opposite end holding two rocks. Place your ear very close to the wire or rod while your friend strikes the rocks together with the wire trapped between. Listen closely for two sounds —one following immediately after the other. The sound is coming through air as well as through the metal. Do sound waves move faster in a gas or a solid?

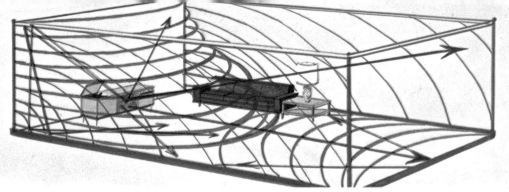

Waves of sound rebounding from all directions cause continuous sound, or reverberation

sound waves traveling in air is too great for the ear, thus causing pain. Human heartbeat is about 10-15 DECIBELS.

Loudness and threshold of audibility are two properties of sound which are important when considering the construction of an auditorium or music hall. However, of greater importance are two other properties known as *interference* and *reverberation.*

Interference has to do with the concentration of sound in certain areas of the hall and no sound at all in other areas. This is a result of one or more echoes combining with other echoes to produce a loud sound, or they may combine and completely cancel each other, thus creating silence.

The second property, reverberation, is much more important than the first. Reverberation is the combining of so many echoes and re-echoes that there is seemingly continuous sound. If the walls and ceiling did not absorb some of the sound, the vibrations would increase into high intensities at times. Fortunately, materials of various natures have different *sound absorbing* qualities. It has been found that it is best to have material of good audience and have most, if not all, of the allowable reverberation set up by the walls near the speaker. When reverberation is present in an auditorium, the speaker seemingly is saying two words at one time because his previous word has not yet been completely absorbed.

According to V. O. Knudson, the maximum time allowable for reverberation is 2.75 seconds. This means that any sound created on the stage should be absorbed completely by an elapsed time of 2.75 seconds. Reverberation time can be reduced considerably by having heavy draperies on the walls, padded seats, acoustical tile on the ceiling, carpet on the floor; and even the presence of the audience affects the total time necessary to mute the sound. A. E. L.
SEE ALSO: ACOUSTICS, OVERTONES, SOUND RECORDING, VOICE

Sound barrier (BARE-ee-ur) The expression "breaking the sound barrier" simply means going faster than the speed of sound in an aircraft.

The problem of calculating the speed of sound was first considered important by Isaac Newton. He attempted to measure it by checking the time lapse between the appearance of flame from a distant cannon burst and the arrival of the report. However, his experiments overlooked the important factor of air temperature and density. It was 130 years later that the French astronomer, Pierre Simon de LaPlace, pointed out this error. Under standard conditions the speed of sound is now accepted to be 760 miles per hour at sea level and 660 miles per hour at an altitude of 35,000 feet.

Supersonic speeds are calculated, beginning with the speed of sound, in *Mach numbers.* Mach 1 stands for the speed of sound; Mach 2 is twice the speed of sound. An aircraft, or any projectile, reaching Mach 1 speed forms a shock wave at its leading edge. A shock wave is a piling-up of air or an accumulation of sound waves. The cannon-like detonation sometimes associated with breaking the sound barrier, or reaching the speed of sound, is really a shock wave generated by an airplane diving at SUPERSONIC speed. As the airplane levels off, the shock wave keeps on going along the original line of flight, hitting the earth with considerable force. The resulting noise is called the *supersonic boom.*

One major difficulty in approaching the speed of sound was a separation of the boundary area, or the thin layer of air normally surrounding an airplane. Such a separation results in a violently-shaking, hard-to-control craft. Now it is known that when a plane is flying at a speed above Mach 1, no boundary layer separation takes place. There is no shaking. E. M. N.

Sound interference (in-tur-FEER-ence) Sound waves move through the air from a source in much the same way that water waves move outward from a stone tossed into a pool. Pressure of an approaching wave of water can be felt, and the lack of push after the wave has passed. The same thing happens to the sound wave: the wave area before the crest is compressed; the area after the crest is *rarefied,* or less dense.

Now if a second stone is dropped in the water at the same spot or at another spot, another series of waves will be started. If these second waves are in phase with the first series, that is, if the compressions of the two sets of waves coincide, and the two sets of rarefactions also, the power of the wave is increased. If these second waves are of the same power and are in opposite phase, that is, if the rarefactions and condensations occur together, they neutralize, or cancel out, one another; and the wave will gradually die out.

Likewise with sound. In sound, when the rarefactions cancel out or neutralize the compressions, silence results. Variations of sound interference occur when the two sets of waves are not exactly in phase or in opposite phase.

Radio men describe another kind of sound interference; a sound of very high *frequency,* such as 15,000 cycles, can be altered by a sound of lower frequency, such as 1000 cycles. Still another phenomenon in sound interference is known as a *zone of silence.* In this situation a sound is heard at its source and vanishes in the distance, only to be heard again farther away. This strange occurrence baffled investigators until one meteorologist discovered that layers of air of different temperatures can deflect sound waves. As sound waves are deflected diagonally upward from warm to cooler air, sound disappears. But if they strike another layer of warm air somewhere above the heads and are deflected earthward again, they may also be received and heard again.　　　　E. M. N.

SEE ALSO: DOPPLER EFFECT, INTERSTELLAR COMMUNICATION, RADIO, RAREFIED AIR, SOUND, SOUND BARRIER

Molecular collision causes absorption or cancellation of sound when the compressions of two sound waves are in opposite phases. The sound wave is lost in this collision.

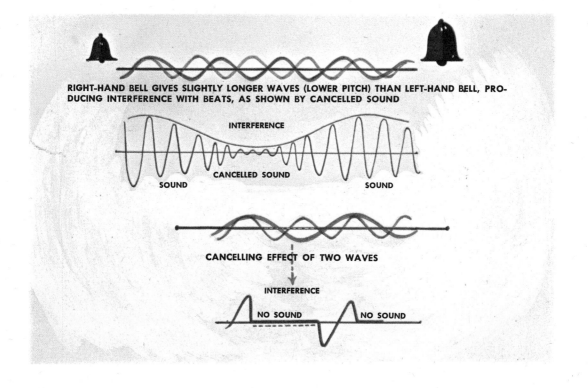

RIGHT-HAND BELL GIVES SLIGHTLY LONGER WAVES (LOWER PITCH) THAN LEFT-HAND BELL, PRODUCING INTERFERENCE WITH BEATS, AS SHOWN BY CANCELLED SOUND

INTERFERENCE

CANCELLED SOUND

SOUND　　　　SOUND

CANCELLING EFFECT OF TWO WAVES

INTERFERENCE

NO SOUND　　NO SOUND

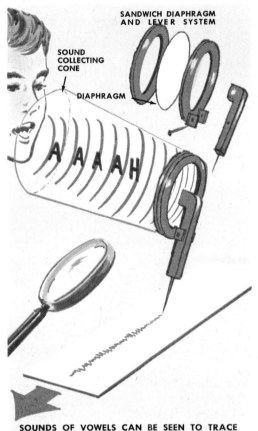

SOUND COLLECTING CONE

DIAPHRAGM

SANDWICH DIAPHRAGM AND LEVER SYSTEM

SOUNDS OF VOWELS CAN BE SEEN TO TRACE DIFFERENT PATTERNS IN A STRIP OF METAL FOIL DRAWN UNDER THE "RECORDING" NEEDLE OF SUCH A DEVICE AS THIS

Sound recording Sound recording, like photography, is a development of modern times. In 1877 Thomas Edison made the first instrument capable of recording and producing sound.

Edison's simple machine consisted of a horn with a diaphragm (a thin, disklike partition that vibrates with sound) at the little end. A cutting needle was attached to the diaphragm. Sound waves, directed at the big end of the horn, struck the diaphragm, causing it to vibrate the cutting needle. In turn the cutting needle etched a groove on a wax-coated, revolving drum. To reproduce the sound, the process was reversed. A needle fol-lowing the groove of the spinning drum vibrated the diaphragm which, in turn, started the sound waves.

In 1887 Emile Berliner replaced the drum with a disk. This acoustical method was able to record only limited frequencies (vibrations) within the band over which the ear can hear.

The development of electron tube amplifiers enabled a wider frequency range of sound to be translated into electric voltage which activated the cutting needles. Upon reproducing the sound, the vibrations of the "play-back" needle are translated into electric voltage which activates a speaker. Tape and wire recordings preserve the sound vibrations magnetically.

In MOTION PICTURES, a tiny fluctuating beam of light creates a narrow path on the edge of sensitive film. In play-back, a beam of light is shined through the modulated strip on the moving film and is changed into electric voltage by a photoelectric cell; the voltage activates a speaker.

Various developments have improved sound recording. In 1948 sound recording companies began issuing "long-play" records. These records revolve more slowly and thus contain more sound. The recording processes and materials were improved so there was much less surface noise. At about the same time, the audio (sound) amplifiers, speakers, and stylus (needle) were improved, resulting in a *high fidelity* (hi-fi) system. A hi-fi system should reproduce accurately over the entire range to which the ear is sensitive, about 20 to 20,000 cycles per second. A large speaker (12 inches or more) called a *woofer* is used for the low frequencies, and a small *tweeter* for the highs. In *stereophonic* recording, two or more microphones are used originally. The signals from the microphones are kept separate on the record and eventually are fed to separate speakers. These speakers should be at least six to eight feet apart. The sound from each speaker originates from the side it would in a concert hall.

Sound transcriptions are used for radio and television programs. Dictating machines and recorders that take phone messages are used in modern offices.   E. M. N.

SEE ALSO: EDISON, THOMAS ALVA

Sounding see Depth sounding, Sonar

A South American rain forest

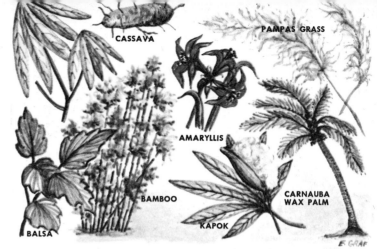

CASSAVA

PAMPAS GRASS

AMARYLLIS

BAMBOO

CARNAUBA
WAX PALM

KAPOK

BALSA

E. GRAF

Some plants native to South America

South America South America, the fourth largest continent, is divided into independent countries and states. It is similar to North America in geological structure and its surface landform pattern. South America is also similar to Africa in its climatic pattern. Both extend about the same number of miles from north to south and both have almost the same shape. Both taper to the south with the southernmost tip pointing to the South Pole. Each has a large expanse of water to the south.

Man probably first reached South America during the Ice Ages. It is thought that he came to the New World across a land bridge between Asia and the North American continent. Then he traveled south, spreading himself through the entire hemisphere.

A number of highly civilized tribes developed in South America. Among these were the Incas. They were concentrated in what is now Peru and Bolivia. The Incas were skilled in both building and agriculture. They were the first people of the New World to practice soil conservation, employing such techniques as crop rotation and terracing. The Spaniards came to this area in the sixteenth century. They claimed the wealth of the Indians and left the natives poor.

Today, South America is a vast and growing continent with a population of more than 137 million.

The world has watched with great interest as Brazil created an entirely new capital, Brasilia, in a remote and thinly populated section.

One of the finest and most beautiful harbors in the world is the famed waterfront of Rio de Janeiro, the former capital, known as one of the really attractive cities of the world.

The so-called "Chicago of Latin America," São Paulo, has now surpassed Rio in population and continues as one of the most rapidly growing and most energetic cities.

LAND FORMS

South America is a great triangle of a continent with the Atlantic Ocean on its eastern shore and the Pacific on the west.

The *Andes Mountains* that follow the western coastline have the highest peaks in all the Americas. This folded and volcanic chain of mountains is the longest in the world, extending north and south for almost five thousand miles. They have been a great barrier to transportation in the history of the continent.

The eastern edge of the continent rises into a plateau region.

The central plain has two great river basins: the Amazon River basin to the north and the Paraná River basin in the south.

CLIMATE

South America has a great variety of climates. They range from the cool, moist cli-

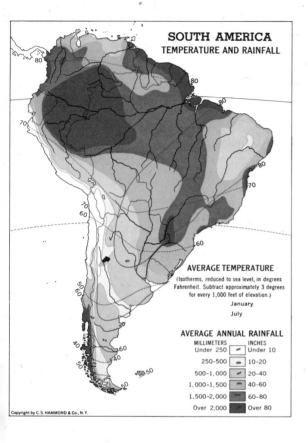

SOUTH AMERICA
TEMPERATURE AND RAINFALL

AVERAGE TEMPERATURE

(Isotherms, reduced to sea level, in degrees
Fahrenheit. Subtract approximately 3 degrees
for every 1,000 feet of elevation.)

January
July

AVERAGE ANNUAL RAINFALL

MILLIMETERS		INCHES
Under 250		Under 10
250–500		10–20
500–1,000		20–40
1,000–1,500		40–60
1,500–2,000		60–80
Over 2,000		Over 80

Copyright by C. S. HAMMOND & Co., N.Y.

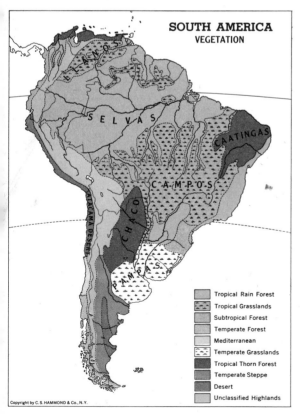

SOUTH AMERICA
VEGETATION

	Tropical Rain Forest
	Tropical Grasslands
	Subtropical Forest
	Temperate Forest
	Mediterranean
	Temperate Grasslands
	Tropical Thorn Forest
	Temperate Steppe
	Desert
	Unclassified Highlands

Copyright by C. S. HAMMOND & Co., N.Y.

mate of the southernmost tip to the great areas of tropical rain forests to the north. There the average temperature is high, and the rainfall is heavy.

In northern Chile there is one of the most barren deserts of the world. Once for a period of fourteen years not a shower fell in this region.

In contrast to this, the extreme southern part of Chile measures its rainfall in feet, not in inches.

The central, fertile valley of Chile is still another contrast. This agricultural region is called the "Garden of South America" and the climate compares favorably with that of central California.

Some of the great variety of climate is due to the differences in altitude of the mountain areas, the plains, plateaus and tropical rain forests. Most of this continent lies within the tropics and the steaming forests are unattractive to European settlers.

RIVERS AND DRAINAGE

South America boasts the most prodigious river system in the world, the *Amazon* with its tributaries.

The Amazon carries more than one-fifth of all the fresh running water of the world. Where it empties into the ocean it pushes the salt water back for 150 miles.

In addition to being part of a great drainage system, the Amazon River is important as a part of the transportation system for moving both goods and men.

Most of Venezuela, at the top of the continent of South America, is drained by the great river, the Orinoco.

Colombia, in the northwest corner of the continent, is drained by the Magdalena River which is called "The Mississippi of Colombia." The greater part of the population of Colombia live along this river.

Where the thick black jungle lands of the Argentine, Brazil and Paraguay blend into one dark mass, the rivers Paraná and Iguassu meet, flowing along together, forming a small part of the boundary lines of these countries. They create the world's most mighty waterfall—Iguassu.

This falls, with the probable 14,000,000 horsepower, more than three times that of Niagara, has great scenic beauty. It is fast becoming a leading tourist attraction.

PLANTS AND ANIMALS

Many Bolivians receive a large part

80°   70°   60°   50°   40°

CARIBBEAN SEA

ATLANTIC

CENTRAL
AMERICA

Panama CANAL ZONE
Canal (to U.S.)
PANAMA

OCEAN

10°

Barranquilla   Maracaibo   Caracas   Trinidad (British)
Port of Spain

Medellín   Orinoco River   Georgetown

VENEZUELA   GUIANA   BRITISH   Paramaribo
Manizales   Angel   GUIANA   SURINAM   Cayenne
Bogotá   Falls   HIGHLANDS   (Dutch)   FRENCH GUIANA

COLOMBIA

Equator

Quito   Belém
Cotopaxi   Rio Negro   São Luis   0°
ECUADOR   Amazon River   River

Guayaquil   Iquitos   Manaus   Amazon   Fortaleza
  Selvas   Cape
Chiclayo   Rio Tapajós   São Roque
  Natal

Trujillo   PERU   Rio Madeira   BRAZIL   Caatingas   Recife
Rio   10°
Branco
Callao   Lima   Huancayo
Cusco   Rio São Francisco   Salvador
  Cuiabá
Illampu   Brasília
Lake   La Paz   Campos
Titicaca   BOLIVIA   BRAZILIAN
Arequipa   Sucre   Campo   Belo Horizonte   HIGHLANDS   20°
Grande
Iquique   PARAGUAY   Rio Paraná   São Paulo   Rio de Janeiro
Asunción   Iguassu   Santos   Tropic of Capricorn
Antofagasta   Gran   Falls   Curitiba
Atacama Desert   Chaco
Tucumán   Rio Uruguay   Pôrto Alegre
Coquimbo   ARGENTINA   Rio Paraná
Córdoba   URUGUAY   30°
Aconcagua   Santa Fe   Rosario
Valparaíso   Mendoza   Montevideo
Santiago   Pampas   Buenos   Rio de la Plata
Juan Fernández   Aires   La Plata
Islands
(Chilean)   Concepción   Bahía   Rio Colorado
Blanca

CHILE   Patagonia

Puerto Montt   40°

Falkland
Islands
(British)

Strait of
Magellan
Punta Arenas   Tierra
del Fuego

Cape Horn   50°

ATLANTIC OCEAN

PACIFIC OCEAN

Map of
SOUTH AMERICA
SCALE OF MILES
0   100   200   300   400   500   600

✪ Capitals of Countries
● Cities
▬▬▬ Boundaries of Countries
▲ Mountain Peaks
〰〰 Canals
〰〰 Falls

Mountains   Highlands   Lowlands   Depression   Water

Copyright by C.S. HAMMOND & Co., N.Y.

Longitude   90°   West of   80°   Greenwich   70°   60°   60°   50°   40°   30°   20°

1—CAPYBARA
2—JAGUAR
3—GUANACO

4—BRAZILIAN TAPIR
5—MARSH DEER
6—ALPACA

SOME ANIMALS OF SOUTH AMERICA

Chicago Natural History Museum

of their support from the LLAMA, a beast like a small camel. The llama supplies wool for clothing, milk, and meat, and carries loads of merchandise from place to place.

More varieties of hummingbirds live in Ecuador than anywhere else in the world. Countless, brilliantly colored birds and strange animals live in the tropical jungles. The rain forests bloom with tropical flowers. So dense is the growth of trees and ferns and other plants that parts of these jungles have not yet been explored.

The variety of plants and animals of South America is as wide as the range of climate of the country. There is everything from tropical snakes, anteaters, jaguars to the king penguins for which the island of South Georgia is famous.

A continent that raises coffee, cacao, sugar cane, cassava, also raises wheat and cotton. The first Irish potatoes grew in Peru, and were only later introduced into Europe.

The cinchona tree found ideal growing conditions in the mountains of Peru. Its bark is the source of QUININE.

The wealth of the jungles of South America remains among the world's least-used treasures. The time may come when the continent's unused resources will be used to help feed the world.

NATURAL RESOURCES

South America is rich in minerals. The Incas made wide use of gold. The Spanish conquerors discovered gold in 1550 and established the famous gold mines at Zaruma.

Most of the world's finest emeralds and much of its platinum have come from Colombia.

Bolivia is one of the richest sources of minerals in the world, but for the most part they have lacked development. This is due in part to the fact that Bolivia no longer has a sea coast from which to ship out her products.

At one time, Chile's greatest wealth came from the huge deposits of nitrate in the northern deserts, but it is not so much in demand now that nitrates are made artificially.

Brazil has the largest undeveloped deposits of iron ore anywhere, and the richest manganese beds. Oil deposits are being opened, but the great potential wealth of this country has scarcely been tapped.

Unlike many South American countries, Venezuela has been able to tap its resources to become a great oil-producing land. Caracas, the capital, and its approaches have been greatly developed by oil wealth of the country.

When the Spaniards came and took the

Photos courtesy Society For Visual Education, Inc.

The agouti (top) is a South American rodent pest that resembles a short-eared rabbit. The marmoset (bottom) belongs to a group of the smallest monkeys

wealth of the Incas and discovered gold, they overlooked one of the great resources of Peru, the deposits made by birds, called *guano,* on the islands off the shore. Protected by law, the guano islands are still worked for their wealth in fertilizer.

Brazil first gave the world rubber and the great boom in rubber made many fortunes until the crash came. Much of the world's coffee comes from this country. Its valley of the San Francisco River is said by many to be as rich as the Mississippi. Cotton, carnauba wax, and hundreds of kinds of cabinet woods are shipped from this country to all parts of the world.

Argentina ranks as one of the world's largest exporters of corn and beef. Often it ships more wheat than Canada and more mutton than New Zealand. The gauchos of Argentina are almost as famous as the U.S. cowboys, and they perform much the same job.

The wealth of Uruguay, a much smaller country than Argentina, is also based on stock raising and meat packing.

The city of Magellanes is the farthest south of any sizeable city in the Americas and is the center for grazing and lumber industries.

South America has great potential wealth in its forests, farms, ranches and mines.

South America has been slow in its de-velopment for many reasons. One of the most important of these is the lack of a suitable transportation system. There are few highways and railroads. Water transportation is limited in many regions. In recent years, the airplane has become a very important means of travel and transport. It has overcome many geographic barriers.

SEE ALSO: EARTH, GEOGRAPHY, NATURAL RESOURCES

South Pole see Poles, North and South

Sow see Pig

Soybean The soybean plant grows to six feet in height. It branches out in all directions. There are three leaflets on each stem. The fruit, a brown hairy bean, grows to three inches on a short stalk and holds two to four black, brown, green or yellow seeds. The small flowers are white or purple.

Soybeans grow well in ordinary, well-drained soil, enriching it with nitrogen. The plant is cut for food for stock, and the valuable bean is removed by threshing. The beans and hulls are ground into a meal, which supplies important protein to hog, chicken, and cattle feeds. Soybean meal is used in some sausage and macaroni products. It is mixed with certain flours or sold as soybean flour.

Thousands of years ago the soybean was thought to be a sacred grain by the Chinese. Today people throughout the world depend upon it for food for themselves and for their animals. Industry uses it in making paints, linoleum, fertilizer, and medicine.

Oil from the bean is used in making margarine, shortening for frying, salad oil, and in the canning of sardines, tuna, and other fish. The soybean has more protein than beef, more calcium than milk and is also rich in vitamins and minerals. A soybean extract is given to babies allergic to cow's milk. P. G. B.

SEE ALSO: LEGUME

Soybean

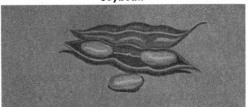